Our Friends in Heaven

Our Friends in Heaven

Saints for Every Day Volume 2
July to December

Written by the Daughters of St. Paul
Edited by Sister Allison Gliot
Illustrated by Tim Foley

Pauline
BOOKS & MEDIA
Boston

Library of Congress Control Number: 2020945551

CIP data is available.

ISBN 10: 0–8198–5522–7

ISBN 13: 978–0-8198–5522–0

Cover and interior design by Mary Joseph Peterson, FSP

Cover art and illustrations by Tim Foley

Published by Pauline Books & Media, 50 Saint Pauls Avenue, Boston, MA 02130–3491

Printed in the USA

OFIH2 VSAUSAPEOILL11-1210170 5522-7

www.pauline.org

Pauline Books & Media is the publishing house of the Daughters of St. Paul, an international congregation of women religious serving the Church with the communications media.

1 2 3 4 5 6 7 8 9   25 24 23 22 21

We would like to dedicate this book to our dear

Sister Susan Helen Wallace, FSP

(1940–2013),

author of the first edition of
Saints for Young Readers for Every Day.
Her joyful spirit and love for the saints
inspired us to pour our own hearts
into this work in the hopes that
it will touch many lives.
From eternity, may she intercede
for all the readers of this new edition.

Contents

August

SEPTEMBER

OCTOBER

NOVEMBER

How to Use this Book

This book is the second volume of a two-part set. Volume I covers January through June. Volume II covers July through December. In these pages, you will find stories about lots of saints. Some lived long lives; others died when they were young. Some were close to God from their childhood and teenage years. Others learned the hard way that only God can make us happy.

There are saints from every part of the world. They lived in many different centuries, from the time of Jesus to our own time. You will come to know saintly kings and laborers, queens and housemaids, popes and priests, nuns and religious brothers. They were mothers and fathers, teenagers and children. They were doctors and farmers, soldiers and lawyers.

Saints are not just one type of person. They were as different from each other as we are. They were as human as we are. They lived on this earth, experienced temptations, and faced problems. They became saints because they used their willpower to make right choices and they prayed. Even when they made mistakes, they never gave up trusting in Jesus' love for them.

You might ask, "What is the difference between a SAINT and a BLESSED?" Saints are holy persons now in heaven who grew close to God while on Earth. The Church declares them saints so that we can love, imitate, and pray to them. Saints can pray to God for us and help us. Persons declared BLESSED are holy people who are now in heaven. Usually the Church requires miracles obtained through their intervention. When the miracles have been carefully studied and accepted as real, the blessed are proclaimed saints.

You will also meet MARTYRS in this book. Martyrs allowed themselves to be put to death rather than deny God or give up their Catholic faith.

Some saints are the PATRONS of particular needs, places, or groups of people. This means that those saints pray in a special way for those things. When you have a specific problem that you need help with, you can ask the patron saint of that problem to pray for you. You can also choose your own special patron saints to turn to in times of need (for example, a saint who shares your name, birthday, or is from the same country as you). These patron saints can become your friends in heaven, helping you throughout your life.

What is the best way to read this book? Do not try to read all the stories in a few days. Read them one day at a time (for example, before you go to bed each night). At the top of each biography, you can find when that saint was alive, which day his or her feast is celebrated on, and what he or she is the patron of. At the end, there is a short prayer to help you get to know the saint better and ask him or her for help in your everyday life.

If you read one story a day, you will have made many new friends in heaven by the end of the year. They will be happy to help you grow closer to God. And maybe someday you will become a saint, too!

NOTE: This book is not intended to be used as a liturgical calendar of Church celebrations. Sometimes, the reading for the saint is on his or her feast day, but not always.

July 1

Saint Junípero Serra

(November 24, 1713–August 28, 1784)

Feast Day: July 1

Patron of California, Hispanic Americans, and vocations to Church ministry

Junípero was born to a farming family on an island off the coast of Spain. He went to a school run by Franciscans. Just before his seventeenth birthday, he joined the Franciscan Order. Junípero was inspired by the life of Saint Francis Solano, a missionary to South America. He decided that, if it was God's will, he would be a missionary too.

Junípero became a priest and a philosophy teacher for the next twenty years. But then he was given a wonderful opportunity. Franciscans were asked to go to the mission territories called "New Spain" (Mexico and California). Junípero and his close friend, Friar Francisco Palou, volunteered. They sailed across the Atlantic Ocean. Then they walked hundreds of miles to Mexico City. During that journey, Junípero got a wound on his leg that never healed. He offered this pain up to Jesus and did not let it stop him from doing the work he felt God calling him to do.

Junípero and Francisco were first sent to live among the Pame peoples in north-central Mexico. Then in 1769, Junípero, Francisco, and a few others were asked to go to

1

the native peoples in Upper California. They made the long journey and started to befriend the Native Americans in that region. Gradually, people were baptized and began to live the Christian faith. Junípero and the friars loved the native peoples. They protected them from other Europeans who wanted to treat them badly. They taught the Native Americans about God, but they also helped them learn new farming and trading techniques. Over the next thirteen years, Junípero and his companions started nine missions in Upper California.

At the end of his life, Junípero traveled a lot between these missions to visit the people there. This was hard for him because of his leg. He was often in pain. Worn out from all his work, he died peacefully when he was seventy. By that time, more than six thousand people in Upper California had been baptized.

Saint Junípero Serra, you thought Jesus was so important that you traveled all over the world to tell people about him. Help me be excited about Jesus, too. Teach me how to share that excitement with others. Amen.

July 2
Saint Elizabeth of Portugal
(c. 1271–July 4, 1336)

Feast Day: July 4

Patron of peace and against war

Elizabeth, a Spanish princess, was born around the year 1271. She was named after her great-aunt, Saint Elizabeth of Hungary. She married King Denis of Portugal when she was twelve years old. At that time, it was more common for royalty to marry at a young age for political reasons. As Elizabeth got older, she was beautiful and very lovable. She was also devout and went to Mass every day. Elizabeth was a charming wife. Her husband was fond of her at first, but soon he began to cause her great suffering. Though he was a good ruler, he did not love prayer and virtue like his wife did. In fact, his sins of impurity were well-known scandals throughout his kingdom.

Elizabeth tried to be a loving mother to her children, Alphonso and Constance. She was also generous and loving with the people of Portugal. Even though her husband was unfaithful, she prayed that he would have a change of heart. Elizabeth refused to become bitter and resentful. She strengthened her own prayer life and followed the Franciscan spirituality. Gradually, the king was moved by her patience and good example. He began to live better. He apologized to Elizabeth and showed her greater respect. In his last sickness the queen never left his side, except for when she went to Mass. King Denis died in 1325. He had shown deep sorrow for his sins and his death was peaceful.

Elizabeth lived eleven more years. She performed loving acts of charity and penance. She was a wonderful model of kindness toward the poor and sick. This gentle woman was also a peacemaker between members of her own family and between nations. When people were ready to go to war, she would step in and help them solve their problems without fighting. Elizabeth died on July 4, 1336. She was at peace because she had spent her whole life loving and serving God and she wanted to be with him forever in heaven.

Saint Elizabeth, you were known as a peacemaker. Please help bring peace to my family and friends. Help me forgive others when I am angry so that I can bring peace to the people around me. Amen.

July 3
Saint Thomas the Apostle
(First Century)

Feast Day: July 3

Patron of India, construction workers, and those who doubt

Thomas was one of the twelve apostles of Jesus. His name means "twin." Thomas loved Jesus greatly, even though at first his belief was not very strong. Once when Jesus was going to face the danger of being killed, the other apostles tried to stop him. Thomas said to them, "Let us also go, that we may die with him" (Jn 11:16). If Jesus was going somewhere, Thomas wanted to be right there with him.

When Jesus was captured by his enemies, Thomas lost his courage. He ran away with the other apostles and was not there when Jesus died. His heart was broken at the death of his beloved Lord. Then on Easter Sunday, Jesus appeared to his apostles after he had risen from the dead. Thomas was not with them at the time. As soon as he arrived, the other apostles told him joyfully, "We have seen the Lord." They thought Thomas would be happy. Instead, he did not believe their story. He said that he would not believe them unless he could put his fingers into the nail marks and wounds on Jesus' body (Jn 20:25).

Eight days later, Jesus appeared to his apostles again. This time, Thomas was there, too. Jesus called him and told him to touch his hands and the wound in his side. Poor Thomas! He fell down at Jesus' feet and cried out, "My Lord and my God!" Then Jesus said, "Have you believed because you have seen me? Blessed are those who have not seen and yet have come to believe" (Jn 20:26–29). Jesus was talking about us, because we believe in him without seeing him. After Pentecost, Thomas was strong in his belief and trust in Jesus. It is said that he went to India to preach the Gospel. He died as a martyr there after sharing the Good News about Jesus with many people.

Saint Thomas, you had questions and doubts, but Jesus answered all of them. Help us to find answers to our questions and to bring our doubts to Jesus when we are not sure about something. Amen.

July 4

Blessed Pier Giorgio Frassati

(April 6, 1901–July 4, 1925)

Feast Day: July 4

Patron of Catholic young adults

Pier Giorgio Frassati was born in Turin, Italy, to a wealthy family. His family expected him to be like his father by becoming a journalist and becoming friends with powerful people in Italy. But Pier Giorgio had other plans. At a very young age, Pier Giorgio learned how to love the poor. He gave his shoes and socks to a beggar when he was only four years old. As he got older, Pier Giorgio liked to give his money away. His father wanted to give him a car when he graduated. Instead, Pier Giorgio wanted to give the money away to the poor and buy medicine for the sick. He tried to show everyone Jesus' love, especially if a person was sick, hungry, or lonely.

His mother had taught him about Jesus, but Pier Giorgio loved Jesus more than she thought possible. He would go to Eucharistic adoration and loved to pray the Rosary. He thought about becoming a priest but decided that God was calling him to do something else. So he became an engineer and told the people he worked with about Jesus.

Pier Giorgio was an ordinary young man. He enjoyed playing jokes on people and laughing with them. On the weekends, he loved to go hiking, mountain climbing, or skiing. Sometimes he went alone so that he could enjoy God's creation quietly. Other times he would go with his friends.

When Pier Giorgio was twenty-four years old, his grandmother became sick. The Frassati family knew that she would die soon. Pier Giorgio himself began to feel very tired and he had trouble leaving bed. But no one realized how sick he was getting until after his grandmother died. They called a doctor, but it was too late. Pier Giorgio died on July 4, 1925. Hundreds of poor people came to his funeral. His parents were shocked because they did not know how much their son had helped others.

Blessed Pier Giorgio Frassati, you showed people Christ's love without drawing attention to yourself. Pray for me, that I will also do acts of kindness out of love for Jesus and others. Amen.

July 5
Saint Anthony Maria Zaccaria
(1502–July 5, 1539)

Feast Day: July 5

Patron of physicians

Anthony was born to a noble family in Italy. His father died before Anthony was old enough to remember him. But Anthony's mother took good care of him and raised him in the faith. From a young age, Anthony felt a special love for the poor. His mother encouraged this. She sent him to the University of Padua so that he could become a doctor. He was only twenty-two when he graduated.

Anthony was a very good doctor. Yet he did not feel satisfied. He realized that he wanted to become a priest. Anthony began to study theology. He also continued to care for the sick and visit the dying, giving them comfort and spiritual guidance. He used all his free time to read the letters of Saint Paul in the Bible. Anthony burned with a strong desire to become a saint and to bring everyone to Jesus, just like Saint Paul did.

After he was ordained a priest, Anthony moved to the great city of Milan. He helped many more people while he was there. He also started an order of priests. They were officially called the Clerics Regular of St. Paul, but everyone called them "Barnabites." This was because the Church of St. Barnabas was their headquarters. In imitation of the Apostle Paul, Anthony and his priests preached everywhere. They explained Paul's message with words that were easy to understand. They also helped the poor, taught the faith, and called people to change their lives by having a relationship with God. Anthony had a great love for Jesus in the Blessed Sacrament. He and his priests spread devotion to Jesus in the Eucharist by teaching others how to pray and go to Eucharistic adoration. Besides the Barnabites, Anthony also founded two other organizations for people who wanted to participate in this mission. One was for women religious and the other was for married people.

After a few years, Anthony became very ill. He was able to visit his mother one last time before he died at age thirty-six.

Saint Anthony, you were a doctor who healed people's bodies, but you also wanted to take care of their souls. Help me remember to say my prayers for the people I love. Amen.

July 6
Saint Maria Goretti
(October 16, 1890–July 6, 1902)

Feast Day: July 6

Patron of teenage girls, victims of crime, and young people

Maria was born to a poor family in Italy. Her father died when she was young. At eleven years old, Maria was already very beautiful. She helped her mother on the farm and in the house, taking care of her five brothers and sisters. She never complained because they were so poor. In fact, she cheered up her mother and was a great comfort to her.

A young neighbor, Alessandro, paid special attention to Maria because she was pretty. He was often very rude to her. She did her best to avoid him. But one hot summer day, when Maria was alone at the house, Alessandro came and tried to force her to do things she did not want to do. She fought against him, telling him that God did not want him to sin. But he would not listen and became very angry. He stabbed her with a knife and ran away. Maria was taken to a hospital, where she died the next day. During her last hours, she forgave her murderer. She said she wanted Alessandro to be with her in heaven someday. With great joy, the girl received Jesus in Holy Communion. Then she died.

Alessandro was sent to prison. For a long time, he did not repent of his horrible crime. Then one night he had a dream or vision of Maria offering him flowers. From that moment on, he was a changed man. When he was freed from prison after twenty-seven years, he went to visit Maria's mother. He asked her for forgiveness, and they went to Mass together the next day. Then Alessandro spent the rest of his life as the gardener at a nearby monastery.

Maria was declared a saint in 1950. Her mother and surviving brothers and sisters were at the celebration.

Saint Maria Goretti, you chose to forgive the man who attacked you. Pray for us to have the grace to choose forgiveness, even when it is very difficult. And when we are hurt by others, may we remember we are beloved children of God. Amen.

July 7
Blessed Peter To Rot
(March 5, 1912–July 7, 1945)

Feast Day: July 7
Patron of Papua New Guinea, catechists, and Christian marriage

Peter To Rot was born on an island in Papua New Guinea. At that time, Christianity was still a new religion on the island. Peter's parents were some of the first to be baptized by the missionary priests. His father was a leader among the native people and helped many to become Catholic. Peter grew up loving his faith and Jesus.

When Peter got older, he knew God was asking him to teach people about God's love. He thought about becoming a priest. Peter's father asked him to wait until he was a little older to make that decision. Peter had a love for the sacrament of marriage, too. Eventually, Peter decided to get married to a woman named Paula la Varpit. They had three children.

Peter became a catechist for his town. He helped the priests teach the faith and helped the people to follow Jesus. In 1942, Japan invaded Peter's island during World War II. The Japanese arrested all of the missionary priests. Peter and the other catechists worked hard to remind the people on the island about God's love while the priests were in prison.

The Japanese army was concerned that the Christians might not follow their rules. They tried to stop Christians from following God. The army encouraged the men on the island to marry more than one woman. Jesus himself reminds us that marriage is between one man and one woman who love each other (Mt 19:3–9). Peter stood up against the Japanese army by encouraging each man to remain faithful to his wife.

The Japanese soldiers arrested Peter for defending God's teaching. They put him in prison in 1945. They realized Peter would never stop encouraging people in the Christian faith. Peter knew that he would die soon. His wife and mother brought him some good clothes, a cross, and a rosary. Then one day, a doctor came and poisoned Peter in his cell. The Japanese army pretended that Peter died from an infection. The other prisoners, however, knew the truth: Peter To Rot had been killed because he loved Jesus.

Blessed Peter To Rot, you knew that God's "rules" help us live happy lives. I want to live a life of joy and love for God! Pray for me, that I will learn how to follow the commandments. Amen.

July 8
Saint Aquila and Saint Priscilla
(First Century)

Feast Day: July 8

Aquila and Priscilla were a married couple who were good friends of Saint Paul. Paul mentions them in three of his letters. He even tells us they risked their lives for him (see Rom 16:3)!

Aquila and Priscilla lived during the time of Jesus, but they never met Jesus in person. Aquila was born in Pontus, in modern-day Turkey. Priscilla was probably born in Rome. We do not know how they met, but we know they were married and living in Rome by the late 40s A.D. During this time, the apostles were eagerly preaching the good news of Jesus' resurrection. When the news arrived in Rome, Aquila and Priscilla heard and believed. They were baptized and began living as followers of Jesus.

In the year 49, Emperor Claudius ordered all Jews and Jewish Christians to leave Rome. Aquila and Priscilla moved to the city of Corinth. A short time later, Paul arrived there to preach the Gospel. Aquila and Priscilla befriended Paul and let him stay with them. Gradually their house became a meeting place where Christians could pray, share their faith, and celebrate the Eucharist together. It was the first "church" in Corinth.

After a few years, Paul left Corinth to preach the Gospel in the city of Ephesus. Aquila and Priscilla went with him. Again, they generously offered their home as a "church" for the Christians there. They also taught many people, including a man named Apollos. Apollos had heard about Jesus and was very excited to preach about him to everyone. However, he only knew little pieces of Jesus' life and teaching. Aquila and Priscilla took the time to help Apollos learn about the rest of the faith. He went on to become a great disciple for Christ.

After Claudius died and Rome was safe again, Aquila and Priscilla returned there. We do not know much about where they went after this. According to one tradition, Aquila was named bishop of Asia Minor. He and Priscilla then spent the rest of their lives serving God's people together. They may even have become martyrs for Christ.

Saints Aquila and Priscilla, you made your home a place where people could learn about Jesus and celebrate their faith together. Help me to share my Catholic faith with others as joyfully as you did. Amen.

July 9

Saint Augustine Zhao Rong and Companions

(died 1648–1930; Augustine: 1746–January 27, 1815)

Feast Day: July 9

Patrons of China, catechists, and missionaries

Augustine Zhao Rong is celebrated with 119 "companions" who died for their Catholic faith in China. These brave men, women, and children lived between the years 1648 and 1930. This was a time when many people in China were suspicious of Christianity. Sometimes their suspicions turned violent. Still, the saints of China stayed faithful to Christ. They knew that nothing—not even suffering—could separate them from God's love.

One of these saints was Augustine Zhao Rong. Zhao was born in 1746 in the Guizhou province in Southwest China. Like most Chinese, he grew up in a non-Christian family. He joined the army at age twenty and worked at the local jail.

When Zhao was twenty-eight, a French priest arrived in Zhao's region to preach the Gospel. His name was Father Jean-Martin Moye. The local officials heard about Father Moye's preaching and arrested him. They took him to the jail where Zhao was working.

Zhao quickly noticed that Father Moye was not like the other prisoners. He was loving, prayerful, and eager to share his faith. Zhao began to ask him questions about Christianity. When the officials released Father Moye, Zhao followed him to learn more. Father Moye baptized Zhao on August 28, 1776 (the feast of Saint Augustine). Zhao took the name Augustine after his new patron.

After his Baptism, Zhao helped Father Moye and his fellow missionaries teach and care for the poor. Everyone was impressed by Zhao's courage and love. Father Moye urged Zhao to become a priest. Zhao studied and was ordained in 1781. The bishop immediately sent him to the neighboring province of Yunnan to serve the people there.

Zhao spent the rest of his life in Yunnan as a priest. In 1815, he was arrested while traveling to someone's house to give them the sacrament of the Anointing of the Sick. Zhao was charged with the "crime" of being Christian. He was beaten and died days later. Zhao was the first Chinese diocesan priest to be killed for the faith.

Saint Augustine Zhao Rong, you were not afraid to ask questions to learn about the Catholic faith. Your questions helped you meet Jesus and discover his love for you. Help me ask good questions to learn more about my faith! Amen.

July 10
Blessed Andrew of Phú Yên
(c. 1624–July 26, 1644)

Feast Day: July 26

Patron of catechists and young people

Andrew was born in the Phú Yên Province of Vietnam. He was the youngest child in a poor family. His mother did her best to raise Andrew and his siblings in the Catholic faith. But this was not easy. At that time, the Vietnamese government wanted to rid the country of Christianity. They persecuted Christians and forbade missionary priests from serving in Vietnam. People like Andrew's mother had to live their faith with no priests, no Mass, and no sacraments.

When Andrew was a teenager, the French Jesuit Alexandre de Rhodes arrived in Phú Yên. Father de Rhodes was on a secret mission to share the faith with the Vietnamese people. He traveled across the country preaching, teaching, and baptizing. Andrew's mother was overjoyed to meet Father de Rhodes. She begged him to teach Andrew, and Father de Rhodes eagerly agreed. He baptized Andrew and his mother. Then he began to train Andrew as a catechist to help teach people about God and the Church.

Andrew was bright and learned quickly. He was eager to share his love for Jesus with the people of Phú Yên and beyond. In 1642, he joined Father de Rhodes and two other catechists on a missionary journey across Vietnam. The little group secretly baptized and taught about one thousand people.

Meanwhile, the Christian persecution was getting worse. Father de Rhodes needed to make sure the Church in

Vietnam would survive if he was exiled or killed. He gathered ten of his catechists, including Andrew, to form a special association. These men made a promise to spend the rest of their lives spreading the Catholic faith.

Andrew's promise was soon put to the test. One year later, a Vietnamese official knocked on his door. He had orders to arrest one of Andrew's fellow catechists. Not finding him, he took Andrew instead. The official brought Andrew before the Vietnamese governor, who ordered him to deny his faith. Andrew refused. He was martyred at age nineteen or twenty. Andrew died saying the name of Jesus. We honor him as the first martyr of Vietnam.

Blessed Andrew, you were proud to confess your love for Jesus, even when it cost you your life. Help me follow your example of courage and faith! Amen.

July 11
Saint Benedict
(c. 480–c. March 21, 547)

Feast Day: July 11

Patron of Europe, cave explorers, and against fever

Benedict and his twin sister, Saint Scholastica, were born in central Italy. They were from a rich Italian family. Benedict was sent to Rome to study in the public schools. But many of the people there were living corrupt lifestyles. Benedict did not want anything to do with that. He left the city and went looking for a place where he could be alone with God. He eventually found a cave in the mountain of Subiaco. Benedict spent three years there, receiving advice and food from a wise monk. The devil often tempted him to go back to his rich home and easy life. However, Benedict overcame these temptations by prayer and penance. During this time, he also grew much closer to God.

Soon, Benedict had such a good reputation that a group of monks asked him to come be in charge of their monastery. But the monks there did not really want to listen to Benedict. They got fed up with his focus on prayer and simplicity. Then they tried to poison him! But God protected Benedict from consuming the poison.

Benedict left those monks and returned to the way he had been living before. But all sorts of people started coming to Benedict for advice. They wanted to learn how to become holy. Some men even wanted to stay with Benedict and imitate his lifestyle. Benedict became the leader of many good monks. He started twelve monasteries. Then he went to Monte Cassino, where he built his most well-known monastery. It was here that Benedict wrote the wonderful rules for his monks. He taught them especially to be humble always and gave them guidance on how to live a holy, well-balanced life. Benedict and his monks greatly helped the people of their times. They taught them how to read and write, how to farm, and how to work at different trades.

After Benedict died, new monasteries continued being founded. Over the centuries, many priests and monks lived by the Rule of Saint Benedict. The Benedictine Order eventually spread all over the world and is still very active today.

Saint Benedict, you liked taking time by yourself to pray, but much of your life was spent in the company of others. Whether I am with lots of people or alone in my room, help me remember to pray often, even something as simple as thinking, "I love you, Jesus!" Amen.

July 12

Saint Louis and Saint Zélie Martin

(Louis Martin: August 22, 1823–July 29, 1894;
Zélie Martin: December 23, 1831–August 28, 1877)

Feast Day: July 12

Patrons of holy marriages, married couples, and family life

Most people know Saints Louis and Zélie Martin as the parents of Saint Thérèse of Lisieux. The Martins show us that holiness belongs to everyone, not just priests and nuns!

Louis and Zélie were born in France. When they were young, they did not know each other. Louis wanted to be a priest and Zélie wanted to become a religious sister. But God had different plans. One day, as Zélie passed a young man on a bridge, she heard God telling her that she would marry that man. She trusted God and, after she and Louis dated for a while, they got married on July 13, 1858.

The Martins poured their whole hearts into God's plan for them: their marriage. Louis and Zélie had nine children together. Sadly, in the span of about four years, four of their children died. The Martins were extremely sad about this, but they continued to trust in God's plan. They raised their other five children, who were all girls, in a loving and faith-filled home.

In 1877, the Martins experienced another hardship. Zélie was re-diagnosed with cancer. By the time they discovered it, there was no medicine that could help her. She did not fear her death. She was scared to leave behind her husband and their five daughters, but she believed that God would take care of them.

After Zélie died, Louis knew that he and his daughters would need loving support. They moved to Lisieux, France, to be close to other family. In Lisieux, several of Louis' daughters decided to enter the convent. It was difficult for him to let go of his daughters, but again, he trusted in God's plan.

Soon, Louis started to show signs that something was wrong with his brain. He spent most of the rest of his life in the hospital. Eventually, he became so weak that he could not walk. Louis died at age seventy-one. The fruits of the Martins' marriage reveal God's ability to do great things with hearts that are open to his plan.

Saints Louis and Zélie Martin, you wanted to become saints, and you wanted the same for your children, so you made a loving, faith-filled home for them. Pray for my family, that we always remember the love of Jesus and show each other his love. Amen.

July 13
Blessed Carlos Manuel Rodríguez Santiago
(November 22, 1918–July 13, 1963)

Feast Day: July 13; May 4 (Puerto Rico)

Carlos Manuel was born in Caguas, Puerto Rico. He was nicknamed Charlie and was the second of five children in a devout Catholic family. When Charlie was six years old, a fire destroyed his home and his father's store. Charlie and his family lost everything and moved in with his grandparents. As Charlie grew up, his grandmother helped him grow in his faith. He also learned from the religious sisters at his school. In time, Charlie received his first Communion and became an altar server. These experiences helped him realize how special the Eucharist and the Mass were. When he went to Mass, he knew he was meeting the God who loved him.

Charlie enjoyed spending time in nature, especially hiking and going to the beach. He also liked his school and graduated at the top of his eighth-grade class. In 1932, Charlie began high school. Then, he got very sick. Doctors discovered he had ulcerative colitis, a serious disease of the digestive system. This painful illness lasted his whole life. Still, Charlie did not complain. He believed that his illness would bring him closer to Jesus. If he suffered with Jesus on the cross, he knew he would also rise with Jesus and live with him forever.

It took Charlie seven years to finish high school. After graduation, he dedicated himself to teaching and writing about the Catholic faith. He printed two magazines and formed discussion groups in parishes. He taught at the

Catholic Center near the University of Puerto Rico. He was a Knight of Columbus and belonged to several other church groups.

Charlie's dream was for everyone to know that God saves us and give us life at Mass. He taught many people about the liturgy and the seasons of the Church, especially Lent and Easter. Charlie wanted people to live these seasons well. He knew they were powerful ways to feel God's saving love.

Charlie died of cancer at age forty-four. He was the first Puerto Rican to be called Blessed.

Blessed Carlos Manuel, you discovered Jesus in the life of the Church. Help me learn more about the Church and the Mass, so I can know Jesus, too! When I struggle to pay attention at Mass, help me focus on what is really happening. Amen.

July 14

Saint Kateri Tekakwitha

(1656–April 17, 1680)

Feast Day: April 17 (Canada); July 14

Patron of ecology and protecting and conserving the environment

Tekakwitha was born in Auriesville, New York. Saint Isaac Jogues and other Catholic missionaries had only come to the area a few years before she was born. Her mother was a Christian Algonquin. Her father was a Mohawk chief who was not Christian. Both her parents died of a disease called smallpox when Tekakwitha was only four. Tekakwitha also got the disease. She survived, but she had scars on her face for the rest of her life.

After that, Tekakwitha was raised by a Mohawk uncle. She did not learn about Christianity until she was eleven years old, when three Jesuit missionaries visited her village. Tekakwitha listened to everything they said about God and Jesus. Then she decided that she wanted to become a Christian, too. She received instructions in the faith and was baptized on Easter Sunday in 1676. That was when she took the name Kateri (a form of Catherine).

Being a Christian made Kateri's life harder in many ways. Her village was not Christian. Her people did not appreciate her choice to remain unmarried. They insulted her, and some resented that she did not work on Sunday. But Kateri loved Jesus and her Catholic faith. She prayed her Rosary every day, even when others made fun of her. She practiced patience and suffered quietly. Soon, however, it became too much. People were treating her so harshly that Kateri had to leave home.

She fled hundreds of miles to a Christian village near Montreal, Canada. For the first time, Kateri could live her faith openly. She was happy to be able to pray and talk about Jesus with other people. She made new friends and received guidance from the Jesuit priests there. They helped Kateri grow in her relationship with God. On Christmas Day in 1677, she joyfully received her first Communion. Her love for Jesus grew even stronger.

Kateri died of an illness when she was around twenty-four years old. After her death, it is said that Kateri's smallpox scars disappeared. Her face became as radiant and beautiful as her soul in heaven.

Saint Kateri Tekakwitha, even though you had to leave your home, you always prayed for your people and brought them to Jesus in your heart. There are many people in our lives who need Jesus, too. Help us to remember them and pray for them today. Amen.

July 15
Saint Bonaventure
(c. 1221–July 15, 1274)

Feast Day: July 15

Patron of children, soap makers, and theologians

Bonaventure was born in Tuscany, Italy. As a young man, he joined the Franciscan Order, which was still very new. He also studied at the University of Paris in France, where he did very well. He became a wonderful teacher and writer about the things of God. But even though his books made him famous, Bonaventure did not brag about his work. He just wanted to help people love God and live their Christian faith.

One of Bonaventure's famous friends was Saint Thomas Aquinas. One day, Thomas supposedly asked Bonaventure where he got all the beautiful things he wrote. Bonaventure pointed to the large crucifix that always stood on his desk. He said that Jesus was the one who taught him everything.

Bonaventure would have been happy to live his life quietly as a Franciscan and an author, but God had other plans in store for him. In 1265, Pope Clement IV wanted Bonaventure to become an archbishop. Bonaventure asked the Pope not to give him such an important position. Then Bonaventure was chosen to be the new head of the Franciscan Order. This time, Bonaventure could not say no. He faithfully carried out this difficult task for seventeen years.

In 1273, Bonaventure became the cardinal and bishop of Albano, Italy. A year later, he went to a big meeting in the Church called the Council of Lyons. Many bishops and

Church leaders were there. Bonaventure helped them solve their problems and everyone was grateful to him. But before the council was over, he died rather suddenly. Bonaventure was later declared a doctor of the Church because of his important writings that helped people grow closer to God.

Saint Bonaventure, you called Jesus your first teacher. You never studied or wrote books without asking him for help first. Whenever I am studying or doing my homework, remind me to say a little prayer before I begin. Amen.

July 16
Saint Marie-Madeleine Postel
(November 28, 1756–July 16, 1846)

Feast Day: July 16
Patron of teachers and students

Julie Postel was born in Normandy, France. She went to a convent school and received a good education. She had the dream of becoming a teacher herself. When she was only eighteen, she opened her own school. But it lasted just five years because hard times were coming to France.

In 1789 the French Revolution started. A new government was set up that was hostile to the Catholic Church. Julie had to shut down her school. Priests who wanted to be loyal to the Pope and the Catholic faith had to go into hiding. Julie helped her pastor to continue his work. She let him use her home to offer Masses in secret. She also secretly brought Holy Communion to sick people. It was a difficult time, but Julie and the faithful Catholics got through it.

When Napoleon came to power in France, he allowed Catholics to practice their faith again. Julie took advantage of this new freedom to go back to teaching. She opened a school in Cherbourg. A few other women came to help her, and they started a new religious order. In 1807 they made their first profession of vows. Julie took the name Sister Marie-Madeleine. The group became known as the Sisters of the Christian Schools of Mercy. They faced many problems, such as misunderstanding by others. At first, the new order did not grow very much. But things changed in 1832. Sister Marie-Madeleine obtained an old convent that she used to expand their mission. More young women started to enter, and the bishop gave his approval to her new order. They helped many children, giving them a good education and teaching them about God. Sister Marie-Madeleine spent the rest of her life teaching and working. She was dedicated to serving God and others to the end.

Saint Marie-Madeleine Postel, you followed Jesus faithfully in good times and in bad. Pray for us that we might not get discouraged when we face difficulties. Help us to follow Jesus and to keep going when problems arise. Amen.

July 17
Saint Leo IV
(c. 790–July 17, 855)

Feast Day: July 17

Leo was a Roman by birth and spent his life in that city. He went to school at the Benedictine monastery near St. Peter's Basilica. As he grew older, he wanted to serve God and his Church. He became a Benedictine monk, and later a priest.

As a priest, Leo was well-known and loved by two popes, Gregory IV and Sergius II. When Sergius died in 847, Leo was chosen to be the new pope. He had a lot of work to do. There were rumors that Rome might be invaded by forces from the Arabian Peninsula. There had already been an attack the year before that had broken down the city walls. Leo had the walls repaired so that it would be harder for enemies to invade. He also started other building projects, rebuilding damaged churches in Rome to make them more beautiful.

Leo did not just take care of church buildings. He took care of people's souls, too. He knew that the people needed good, holy priests to guide them. So he started a renewal program for the clergy. In 853 he called a meeting for all the Roman priests. He gave them rules to help them live more joyful, prayerful lives. That way, they could better serve their parishioners. Leo also loved the beautiful prayers of the liturgy. He encouraged liturgical chant and music because he knew this would help everyone lift their hearts up to God.

As Pope, Leo had to deal with many problems from bishops and political leaders around the world, who would often get into arguments. This was difficult for Leo, but he always tried to respond with patience and love. He did his best to resolve the conflicts and entrusted the rest to God. That was Leo's way of serving Jesus and the Church.

Leo carried out his duties as Pope faithfully right up to the end of his life. He was in his sixties when he died.

Saint Leo IV, you had to handle many challenges during your life. You solved them one step at a time, trusting in God the entire time. When we feel overwhelmed by our problems, help us to stay calm and ask God to be with us. Amen.

July 18
Saint Camillus de Lellis
(May 25, 1550–July 14, 1614)

Feast Day: July 18

Patron of doctors, nurses, and health-care workers

As a boy, Camillus had a rough character. His mother sometimes found him difficult to handle. Then, she died when he was twelve. Four years later, at the age of sixteen, he became a soldier like his father. Like most soldiers of that time, Camillus led an immoral life. He was especially addicted to gambling. When his father died, Camillus became a drifter. He kept gambling a lot. But then he had to go to a hospital in Rome to get treatment for a leg wound, and he started working at the hospital.

His old habits were still with him, and he got into trouble because of his bad temper and rough ways. Camillus tried to improve himself and even thought about becoming a friar. He went to a Capuchin monastery and offered to do manual labor for the friars. Being in this environment was good for him and led him to a complete conversion of life. Back at the San Giacomo hospital in Rome, he began more intense efforts to take care of the sick. Camillus got to know Saint Philip Neri and the saint became his spiritual director. When Camillus was thirty-four years old, he was ordained a priest.

Taking care of the sick was his heart's desire. Camillus decided to begin a new congregation for this purpose. It was known as the Clerics Regular, Ministers of the Sick. Many young men wanted to join Camillus. With great dedication they nursed the poor victims of the plague. They wore a large red cross on their habit. The work continued to flourish, and Camillus constantly cared for the sick people. After he died, the congregation continued to grow and spread throughout the world.

Saint Camillus, you often said that you wanted to help the sick in the same way that a mother would care for her sick child. Pray for us that we might have the same compassion for those whom we are called to serve. Amen.

July 19
Blessed Pavel Peter Gojdič

(July 17, 1888–July 17, 1960)

Feast Day: July 17

Peter was born in Slovakia into a Byzantine Rite Catholic family. His father was a priest (in the Byzantine Rite, priests are allowed to marry). Peter decided to become a priest too, as did his brother Cornelius. They were both ordained on August 27, 1911.

Peter worked in a parish and also did some teaching. Besides that, he worked for the bishop in the diocesan offices. Although Peter liked being a parish priest, he felt that God was calling him to be a monk. After much prayer, he entered the Basilian Order in 1922.

As a monk he took the name Pavel (a form of Paul). He was very devoted to Eucharistic prayer and spent long hours before Jesus in the tabernacle. He was devoted to the Sacred Heart of Jesus, as well as to the Blessed Mother. In 1927 Pavel was appointed to be a bishop. He was well formed to deal with the difficult times that were about to come to Europe.

In the 1930s, a man named Hitler rose to power in Germany and began to persecute the Jews. This affected Slovakia too. Bishop Pavel defended the Jews against the growing hatred toward them. After World War II broke out, Pavel did his best to help those who were suffering, especially refugees and prisoners. The people spoke of him as the man with a heart of gold.

After the war, the communists took over in Slovakia and began to persecute the Catholics. They tried to force Pavel to become Russian Orthodox instead of Catholic. But Pavel refused because he wanted to stay Catholic and be in union with the Pope. In 1950 Pavel was arrested and thrown in jail because of his heroic witness to the Catholic faith. After a mock trial, he was sentenced to life in prison, where the conditions were very harsh. He eventually died of cancer at age seventy-two.

Blessed Pavel, your Catholic faith was the most important thing in your life. You refused to give it up even though you suffered for it. Pray for us that we might always love our Catholic faith and never give it up. Amen.

July 20
Saint José María Díaz Sanjurjo
(October 26, 1818–July 20, 1857)

Feast Day: July 20

José was born into a devout family in Spain. From a young age he felt the desire to become a priest. When he was only ten years old, he was sent to a school to study Latin and other subjects that would help him reach that goal. Then when he was about twenty-four years old, he decided to enter the Dominican Order. He was ordained to the priesthood a few years later.

José wanted to be a missionary and he was soon sent to Manila in the Philippines. He taught there for a short while, but then he was sent to Vietnam. It was not easy to be a missionary in Vietnam. The language was hard to learn, but José picked it up quickly. He also had to get used to the tropical climate, which at times was very hot and humid. But the biggest problem was that Christians in Vietnam were persecuted by the government. There were times of persecution during the eighteenth and nineteenth centuries. It is estimated that about three hundred thousand Christians were martyred during these times.

The persecution was worse at some times than at others, and during José's first years in Vietnam, there was enough peace that he could do a lot of pastoral work. He baptized people, taught them about the faith, and provided the other sacraments for the Catholics there. He also spread devotion to Mary because he was very devoted to her. After a few years of working in Vietnam, he was made a bishop there. But around that time, Emperor Tu-Duc began another persecution. José wrote a pastoral letter to his people urging them to be loyal to the faith. Before long, José was arrested and spent two months in jail. Then he was condemned to death. On July 20, 1857, the sentence was carried out and he was beheaded.

Saint José, you willingly gave your life for Jesus Christ rather than deny the faith. Pray for us, so that we may be grateful for the gift of faith and always live in a way that shows we are Christians. Amen.

July 21
Saint Lawrence of Brindisi
(July 22, 1559–July 22, 1619)

Feast Day: July 21

Lawrence was born in Brindisi, Italy. As he was growing up, he was taught by Capuchin Franciscans. They made such a deep impression on Lawrence that he decided to join the Capuchin Order when he was sixteen. Then he was sent to the University of Padua to study theology. His brother Capuchins had not realized how brilliant Lawrence was. He had a knack for learning languages and could speak at least eight fluently. He also studied the Bible. All these skills came in handy later on in Lawrence's life.

After Lawrence was ordained a priest, he became a popular preacher. Because he could speak Hebrew, he worked with the Jewish population in Rome, telling them about Jesus. Later on, he started many new Capuchin houses around Europe. He also held important jobs in his religious order.

Besides all this, Lawrence was an excellent diplomat. Political leaders would invite him to come make peace and settle disputes for them. He did this successfully in Germany and Spain. Once, Emperor Rudolf II of Austria asked Lawrence for help. An army from Turkey was going to invade, and Rudolf needed the German princes to unite together. Lawrence convinced the princes to fight on Rudolf's side, but they would not go to war without Lawrence. They asked him to stay with them as their chaplain. When the soldiers saw how large the Turkish army was, they wanted to quit. So Lawrence himself rode in the lead.

Legends say he was armed only with a crucifix. The Christian soldiers took heart when they saw Lawrence's bravery. They fought hard and the Turks were completely defeated.

Eventually, Lawrence's many travels and responsibilities started to weigh on his health. He became very sick and died on his birthday when he was sixty years old.

Saint Lawrence of Brindisi, you studied hard in school and God put all your knowledge to use later on. Help us to appreciate our education. May we study well now so that we are ready to follow God's plan wherever it takes us. Amen.

July 22

Saint Mary Magdalene
(First Century)

Feast Day: July 22

Patron of gardeners, hairdressers, and pharmacists

Mary Magdalene was from Magdala, near the Sea of Galilee. Some people identify her as a well-known sinner whom we hear about in the Gospels. It seems that Mary was very beautiful and very proud. But after she met Jesus, she felt great sorrow for her sins. When Jesus went to supper at the home of a rich man named Simon, Mary came to weep at his feet. Then, with her long, beautiful hair, she wiped his feet dry and anointed them with expensive perfume. Some people were surprised that Jesus let such a sinner touch him. But Jesus could see into Mary's heart. He said her sins had been forgiven and that was why she was showing him such great love. Then he told Mary, "Your faith has saved you; go in peace" (Lk 7:50).

From then on, Mary became a follower of Jesus. She traveled with the other holy women who humbly served Jesus and his apostles during their journeys. When Jesus was crucified, she did not run away like many of the apostles did. She was there at the foot of the cross, staying with Jesus even as he took his last breath.

After Jesus' body had been placed in the tomb, Mary was very sad. On Easter morning, she went to anoint Jesus' body with spices. She was shocked when she saw that the tomb was empty. She started to cry, thinking someone had stolen Jesus' body. Suddenly, she saw someone whom she assumed was the gardener. She asked him if he knew where the body had been taken. Then the man spoke in a voice she knew so well: "Mary!" (Jn 20:16) It was Jesus himself, standing right there in front of her. He had risen from the dead. Mary was the very first one to see Jesus after his resurrection.

Jesus sent Mary to announce the good news of the resurrection to Peter and the other apostles. She spent the rest of her life telling others about Jesus and all the wonderful things he had done.

Saint Mary Magdalene, you loved Jesus with your whole heart. This made you brave, and you boldly proclaimed the Good News of Jesus to everyone. Show me how to share that same Good News in my own way today. May I be courageous and loving like you. Amen.

July 23
Saint Bridget of Sweden
(c. 1303–July 23, 1373)

Feast Day: July 23

Patron of Europe, Sweden, and widows

Bridget was born in Sweden to a well-off Catholic family. From the time she was a child, she was greatly devoted to the passion of Jesus and his sufferings on the cross. One day, Bridget seemed to see Jesus on the cross and hear him speak to her. After this experience, she was determined to help everyone love Jesus more.

When she was a teenager, Bridget married a young man named Ulf. Like Bridget, Ulf had set his heart on serving God. Bridget and Ulf loved each other very much and had eight children together. One of them also became a saint, Saint Catherine of Sweden. Bridget and Ulf served at the Swedish royal court. Bridget was the queen's personal maid. She tried to help King Magnus and Queen Blanche lead better lives. For the most part, they did not listen to her, but Bridget still tried her best.

All her life, Bridget had marvelous visions and received special messages from God. She felt God asking her to share those messages with many rulers and important leaders in the Church. Bridget would travel to meet those people and humbly explain what God had told her.

After her husband died, Bridget put away her rich clothes. She lived as a poor nun, totally dedicated to God and prayer. Later, she started the Order of the Most Holy Savior, also known as the Brigittines. She still kept up her own busy life, traveling about and doing good everywhere. Throughout all this activity, Jesus continued to reveal many secrets to her. This did not make Bridget proud, though. It only made her love God more.

Shortly before she died, Bridget went on a pilgrimage to the Holy Land, where Jesus was from. She had visions of what Jesus had said and done in those places. She wrote them down, and they were published after her death.

Bridget died in Rome when she was around seventy years old.

Saint Bridget of Sweden, God gave you many special prayer experiences. We may not hear Jesus speak the way you did, but we can still learn how to hear his voice in our lives. Teach us how to remain faithful to prayer, even when we feel like nothing is happening. Amen.

July 24

Saint Charbel Makhlouf

(May 8, 1828–December 24, 1898)

Feast Day: July 24

Patron of Lebanon

Youssef Makhlouf was born in a mountain village in Lebanon. As he was growing up, he attended the small school and the parish church. He loved the Blessed Mother and he loved to pray. He had two uncles who were monks. Youssef wanted to be a monk, too. Although he did not tell anyone, he prayed to ask Mary for help in becoming a monk.

Youssef's family did not know about this. They wanted him to get married. There was a nice girl in the village who they thought would make an ideal wife. But Youssef believed it was time to follow his call to become a monk. He joined the monastery of Our Lady of Maifouk at the age of twenty-three. After a year, he moved to the monastery of St. Maron in Annaya, Lebanon. He took the name Charbel, after an early martyr with that name. Then he studied to become a priest and was ordained in 1859.

Charbel remained at his monastery for many years. From time to time he would go to stay at the order's hermitage. There, he could be alone with God and devote himself more fully to prayer without any distractions. During the last twenty-three years of his life, Charbel decided to live at the hermitage all the time. He chose to lead a very hard life. He made sacrifices, ate little, slept on the hard ground, and prayed long hours. This helped him remember what was really important in life.

As the years passed, Charbel became a person totally in love with Jesus. Then as he celebrated the Mass on December 16, 1898, he suffered a stroke. Charbel died eight days later on Christmas Eve. Not long after, miracles began to happen at his grave.

Saint Charbel Makhlouf, you lived a quiet, simple life structured around prayer. This brought you great peace and happiness. Teach me how to put aside quiet time every day, even if it is only for a few minutes, so that I can practice listening to God's voice in prayer. Amen.

July 25

Saint James the Greater

(Unknown–44)

Feast Day: July 25

Patron of pharmacists, sailors, and veterinarians

James was a fisherman, along with his father Zebedee and his brother Saint John. He was on his father's boat mending his nets one day when Jesus passed by. Jesus called James and John to follow him. The two brothers left their boat and became Jesus' disciples.

James was a special companion of Jesus, along with John and Saint Peter. The three of them were allowed to see what the other apostles did not see. James watched as Jesus raised the daughter of Jairus from the dead. He went up the mountain to see Jesus' transfiguration, when Jesus shone like the sun with his robes white as snow.

The night before Jesus died, he asked James, Peter, and John to stay with him as he prayed in the Garden of Gethsemane. Jesus was praying very intensely, but the apostles fell asleep. Then James and the others ran away in fear when Jesus was arrested. James was not at the foot of the cross when Jesus died. But after Jesus' resurrection, James was in the Upper Room when Jesus appeared to the apostles. Jesus came through the locked door and said, "Peace be to you" (Jn 19:19). Later, James was there with the other disciples at Pentecost when they received the gift of the Holy Spirit.

In the beginning, James was an impulsive, outspoken man. He asked Jesus bluntly for a seat of honor in his kingdom. He demanded that Jesus send fire down on the villages that did not welcome him. But he also had great faith in Jesus. Eventually, James learned how to become humble and gentle. In the end, he received his "seat of honor" in the kingdom of heaven by becoming the first apostle to die for Jesus. King Herod Agrippa had James put to death by the sword. As a martyr, James gave the greatest witness of all.

Saint James, you were not always perfect, but Jesus still chose you as his close friend. Teach us how to admit our mistakes and ask for forgiveness when we have done something wrong. Help us become good friends of Jesus. Amen.

July 26

Saint Anne and Saint Joachim
(Unknown–First Century)

Feast Day: July 26

Patrons of grandparents; Anne: Patron of Canada

According to tradition, Anne and Joachim were the parents of the Blessed Virgin Mary and the grandparents of Jesus. Most of what we know about them has been passed down through legends and stories over the centuries.

Anne and Joachim probably lived in Bethlehem and Nazareth, the same places where Jesus was born and grew up. They were a happily married couple. They spent their lives worshipping God and doing good for the people around them. They had one great sorrow, however: God had not sent them any children.

For years and years, Anne prayed and begged God to give her a child. She promised to dedicate the baby to him. Then, when Anne was already old, God answered her prayer in a far better way than she could ever have imagined. The child born to Joachim and Anne was the Immaculate Virgin Mary. This holiest of all women was later to become the Mother of God.

Anne and Joachim were overjoyed to have a daughter. Anne took loving care of little Mary for a few years. Then she gave Mary up to the service of God, as she had promised she would. Mary went to stay at the holy Temple of Jerusalem. Anne and Joachim knew that she would be happy there living so close to God. After that, they continued their lives of prayer until God called them home to heaven.

Christians have always been especially devoted to Anne, the grandmother of Jesus. Many beautiful churches have been built in her honor. Perhaps one of the most famous is the Shrine of Saint Anne de Beaupré in Canada. Great crowds go there all year round to ask for Saint Anne's help in their sufferings.

Saint Anne and Saint Joachim, you had to wait a long time for God to answer your prayers, but you never stopped trusting in him. Help us to trust God like you did and have faith that he will answer our prayers when the time is right. Amen.

July 27
Blessed Titus Brandsma
(February 23, 1881–July 26, 1942)

Feast Day: July 27

Patron of journalists

Titus Brandsma was born into a devout family in Friesland, the Netherlands. When he was seventeen years old, he felt God calling him to enter religious life. He became a Carmelite priest and taught at the Catholic University of Nijmegen. His students liked him because he cared about them and explained things well. Titus had a warm, caring heart, and the plight of poor people moved him. He was very generous in helping those in need. He became a journalist and promoted Catholic literature. He knew that the press was an important way to spread the Gospel.

But difficult times were coming to his country. In 1940, the Nazis came from Germany to take over Holland. We know that every person is created with dignity and loved by God. But the Nazis did not recognize this. They did many bad things to certain groups of people. They wanted to spread their wrong ideas through the Dutch newspapers. But the Dutch bishops refused to publish Nazi propaganda in Catholic newspapers. Titus supported the bishops' policy, even though he knew it could get him into trouble with the Nazis. He even took a leading role in opposing the Nazis by delivering a letter from the bishops to the Catholic newspaper editors. Because of this, on January 19, 1942, Titus was arrested and imprisoned.

Titus was sent to the concentration camp at Dachau, Germany, on June 19. The guards often beat him and left him bleeding in the mud. Yet Titus tried to inspire and encourage fellow prisoners. His health broke down under the terrible conditions in the camp. He had to go to the camp hospital, where the Nazis used him for medical experiments. Finally, they killed him with a lethal injection on July 26, 1942.

Saint John Paul II beatified him on November 3, 1985. Titus is recognized as a martyr for the faith because he was killed for defending the Church's freedom and standing up for what he knew was right.

Blessed Titus, pray for us that we will have the courage to face the difficulties of life. Never let us doubt Jesus' love for us. Amen.

July 28
Saint Alphonsa
(August 19, 1910–July 28, 1946)

Feast Day: July 28

Patron of India and against foot problems and diseases

Saint Alphonsa was born into a noble family in Kerala, India. The family belonged to the Syro-Malabar Rite of the Catholic Church. She was baptized Anna but was affectionately called Annakutty. Her mother died when Anna was only three months old, so her father asked his mother to help raise the child. Anna's grandmother loved to tell Anna stories about the saints. In particular, Anna loved to hear about Saint Thérèse of Lisieux. She would pray to Saint Thérèse to know what God wanted her to do with her life.

When Anna was about ten years old, she was put into the care of an aunt. The aunt was very strict in the way she raised Anna, and the girl suffered a lot from her harshness. As she got older Anna knew that God was calling her to become a nun. But her aunt had decided that Anna should get married. In those days, marriages were arranged by the family. Despite all the pressure, Anna stood her ground. In the meantime, she also had an accident when she fell into a burning pit and her feet were badly burned. She never fully recovered from this and had problems with her feet for the rest of her life.

Against all odds, Anna prevailed and entered the religious life. She went to a convent of the Franciscan Clarist Congregation. First, she studied for a while in order to earn a teaching diploma. On August 2, 1928, she officially entered the community and took the name Alphonsa. She became a very fervent nun. She was full of love for Jesus and wanted to offer him all her love. But her health was poor and she began to suffer from many different ailments. Through all of these sufferings, she offered everything to Jesus. She never complained, even when the others did not understand what she was going through.

Alphonsa was only thirty-five years old when she died. People began to pray through her intercession and many miracles happened. She became the first native Indian woman to be declared a saint.

Saint Alphonsa, you are a good model of how to follow Jesus even in the difficulties of life. Pray for us that we may not lose hope in difficult times. Help us to love and follow Jesus each day of our lives. Amen.

July 29

Saint Martha

(Unknown–c. 84)

Feast Day: July 29

Patron of cooks, hotel employees, and painters

Martha was the sister of Mary and Lazarus. They lived in the little town of Bethany near Jerusalem. They were dear friends of Jesus, and he often came to visit them. In fact, the Gospel tells us, "Jesus loved Martha and her sister and Lazarus" (Jn 11:5). It was Martha who lovingly served Jesus when he visited them.

One day, Martha was preparing a meal for Jesus and his disciples. It was a lot of work to take care of that many guests. Martha watched her sister Mary sitting quietly at Jesus' feet, listening to him. Martha complained, "Lord, do you not care that my sister has left me to do all the work by myself? Tell her then to help me" (Lk 10:40). Jesus replied gently, "Martha, Martha, you are worried and distracted by many things; there is need of only one thing. Mary has chosen the better part" (Lk 10:41–42). Jesus was very pleased with Martha's loving service. However, he wanted her to know that listening to God's Word and praying was even more important.

Later on, Martha's great faith in Jesus was seen when her brother Lazarus died. As soon as Martha heard that Jesus was coming to Bethany, she went out to meet him.

She was upset about her brother dying, but she still trusted in Jesus. Jesus told her that Lazarus would rise. He said, "Those who believe in me, even though they die, will live . . . Do you believe this?" (Jn 11:25–26). And Martha answered, "Yes, Lord, I believe that you are the Messiah, the Son of God" (Jn 11:27). Then Jesus worked a great miracle and raised Lazarus from the dead!

Not much is known about Martha's life after Jesus' resurrection and ascension into heaven. According to some traditions, she traveled to many places, sharing the Good News about Jesus with everyone she met.

Saint Martha, you were not afraid to tell Jesus when you thought something was unfair, but you had to learn that you were not always right. When someone corrects me, help me to accept their advice with an open heart, just like you listened to Jesus. Amen.

July 30

Blessed Solanus Casey

(November 25, 1870–July 31, 1957)

Feast Day: July 30

Bernard Francis Casey was born on a farm in Wisconsin. His parents were Irish immigrants who worked hard to provide for their large family. Bernard had little formal education. In 1887 he left the farm and got different jobs. He worked as a prison guard, a lumberjack, and a streetcar operator. He began to think about what God wanted him to do with his life. Soon, the idea of the priesthood came into his heart and he entered a minor seminary. However, the classes were taught in German and Latin, and Bernard did not know those languages. He struggled and did poorly in school. His advisors told him he that he could enter a religious order instead.

When Bernard was trying to decide what order to join, he was praying and heard the Blessed Mother tell him to go to Detroit. The Capuchins, a Franciscan group, were in Detroit. Bernard was accepted. He still did not do well in his studies, so the superiors decided that he could be ordained a "simplex" priest. This meant that he was allowed to celebrate Mass but could not hear confessions or preach during the Mass. Bernard humbly accepted this. He only wanted to serve God and to bring the love of Jesus to all.

As a religious, Bernard took the name Solanus. He was given only simple tasks to do, such as answering the door. But the people loved him because he treated everyone who came to the monastery as if they were Jesus himself. He listened patiently to their stories. He gave good advice to those who were looking for some counsel. And he had a great devotion to the Mass. Solanus told people the benefits of having Masses offered for their intentions. He enrolled them in what was called the Seraphic Mass Association. Crowds of people would come to the monastery looking for Solanus. Over the years, many people were healed through his prayers.

When Solanus died, about twenty thousand people came to pay their respects. Through his humility and prayers, he had touched countless lives.

Blessed Solanus Casey, you did little jobs for Jesus with great love, and this touched the lives of many people. Help me do my little tasks and chores with great love. Amen.

July 31
Saint Ignatius of Loyola
(December 24, 1491–July 31, 1556)

Feast Day: July 31

Patron of Spain, children, and soldiers

Ignatius was from a Spanish noble family. As a boy, he was sent to be a page at the royal court. He dreamed of becoming a great soldier and marrying a beautiful lady. When he was a young man, he fought courageously in the Battle of Pamplona. However, a wound from a cannonball forced him to spend months in bed at Loyola Castle. Ignatius asked for some books to read. He preferred stories of knights, but only biographies of Jesus and the saints were available. Gradually, these books began to make an impression on him. Ignatius wondered if he could do great things the way the saints had. All the fame and glory he had wanted before seemed worthless in comparison.

Ignatius began to imitate the saints in their prayers, sacrifices, and good works. He started to listen to God and have more of a relationship with him. Soon, Ignatius felt called to share Christianity with others in a more intentional way. But to do that well, he had to go back to school and study Latin grammar. It was embarrassing at times, since Ignatius was thirty-three and the other students were young boys. Yet Ignatius did not quit. He knew he would need this knowledge to help him in his ministry.

After he had finished grammar school, Ignatius went to the University of Paris. There he made many friends, such as Saint Francis Xavier and Saint Peter Faber. They liked to discuss God and pray together. Eventually, they felt inspired to start a new religious order called the Society of Jesus. The group of six chose Ignatius to be their leader. They promised to work for God in whatever way the pope thought best.

Ignatius professed his religious vows in 1534 and was ordained a priest four years later. In 1540, the Society of Jesus was officially recognized by the Pope. The members of the Society of Jesus (also called Jesuits) taught the faith, preached, and established schools. The new order grew quickly. By the time Ignatius died at age sixty-four, there were one thousand members.

Saint Ignatius of Loyola, you and your friends traveled together on your journey toward holiness, accomplishing things you never could have dreamed of doing alone. Help me to be a good friend to others. Teach me how to love my friends and pray for them. Amen.

August 1

Saint Alphonsus Liguori

(September 27, 1696–August 1, 1787)

Feast Day: August 1

Patron of confessors, moral theologians, and people suffering from arthritis

Alphonsus was born near Naples, Italy. He was the son of a navy captain. Alphonsus was a hardworking student. He received his degree in law and became a famous lawyer. But a mistake he made in court convinced Alphonsus of what he had already thought: instead of being a lawyer, he should become a priest. His father tried to talk him out of it. However, Alphonsus could not ignore what God was calling him to do.

After he was ordained a priest, Alphonsus' life was filled with activity. He took care of the poor and preached to people about Jesus. He wrote over one hundred books and pamphlets on religious topics. He offered wise spiritual direction and brought peace to people through the sacrament of Reconciliation. He also started a religious congregation called the Redemptorists, who helped the poor and gave them spiritual nourishment. Besides all this, he wrote hymns, played the organ, and painted pictures.

When the Pope wanted to make him a bishop, Alphonsus was so humble that he declined. But the Pope helped

Alphonsus understand that the Church needed good bishops and that God also wanted this. So Alphonsus accepted. As bishop, Alphonsus sent many preachers all over his diocese. The people needed to be reminded of the love of God and the importance of their religion. Alphonsus told the priests to preach simple sermons that everyone could understand, no matter what level of education they had.

As he got older, Alphonsus suffered from illnesses. He had painful arthritis and became crippled. He grew deaf and almost blind. He also had disappointments and temptations. But he had great devotion to the Blessed Mother, and this helped him get through it all. His troubles were followed by great peace and a holy death when he was ninety years old. Alphonsus was proclaimed a doctor of the Church in 1871.

Saint Alphonsus Liguori, you used all your time to do God's work and grow in love for him. You did not waste even a single moment of the time God gave you. Help me remember to set time aside every day to say my prayers and talk to God. Amen.

August 2
Saint Peter Julian Eymard
(February 4, 1811–August 1, 1868)

Feast Day: August 2

Patron of Eucharistic adoration and devotion

Peter was born in a small town in France. He worked with his father, making and repairing knives, until he was eighteen. Peter spent his free hours studying. He taught himself Latin and received instruction in the faith from a helpful priest. He wanted to become a priest, but his father wanted him to stay home and help with the family business. But after his father died when Peter was twenty-three years old, he was able to join a new religious order called the Marists and was ordained. He served as the spiritual director of their seminarians and later became a superior. He traveled many places to give retreats and teach people about the faith.

But Peter is most remembered for his great love of the Eucharist. He loved to spend time every day in adoration before the Blessed Sacrament. He knew Jesus is truly present in the Eucharist, and that was where he heard God most clearly in prayer. He felt how much Jesus loves us by being with us in the Eucharist. He wanted everyone to know about this love and experience it themselves. In 1856, he felt God calling him to start a new religious order of priest-adorers of the Holy Eucharist. They became known as the Congregation of the Blessed Sacrament. Two years later, he helped start an order of sisters, the Servants of the Blessed Sacrament. Like the priests, these sisters had a special love for Jesus in the Holy Eucharist. They devoted their lives to adoration of Jesus. Peter also started parish organizations to help prepare people to receive first Communion. He wrote books on the Eucharist that are still read today.

Peter spent the last four years of his life in severe pain. He also suffered because of difficulties and criticism. But he continued his life of adoring the Eucharist. His witness and sacrifice helped many others find their call in his religious orders and come to love Jesus in the Eucharist. He died at the age of fifty-seven.

Saint Peter Julian Eymard, you wanted everyone to know that Jesus is truly present in the Eucharist and that he loves each of us. Help me pay attention during Mass and always remember how much Jesus loves me. Amen.

August 3

Blessed Stanley Rother
(March 27, 1935–July 28, 1981)

Feast Day: July 28

Stanley was born in Okarche, Oklahoma, in 1935. The Rothers were hardworking farmers with deep faith. They went to daily Mass and prayed the Rosary every evening.

Stanley and his siblings also attended Catholic school. Their life of faith and prayer helped Stanley hear God's call to become a priest.

Stanley entered the seminary after high school. But he was not a strong student. His grades were so low that the seminary asked him to leave. Stanley approached the bishop for help. When the bishop saw how determined Stanley was, he gave him another chance. Stanley entered another seminary and was ordained in 1963.

Stanley served as a priest in Oklahoma for five years. Then God put a new desire in his heart. His diocese had a mission church in Guatemala. The church was in a poor, rural area. The people there had not had their own priest for nearly one hundred years. Stanley wanted to serve them. He asked his bishop for permission to move to Guatemala and help with the mission. The bishop agreed.

Stanley loved the Guatemalan people. They were farmers, like he was. It was easy for him to connect with them. Even though he struggled with languages, he learned Spanish and the native Tz'utujil language. Stanley celebrated Mass, cared for the sick, and helped the people farm. He fixed their cars and played with the children. He shared their poor, hardworking way of life.

Stanley also saw great suffering. Guatemala was at war. Violence erupted between the people and their government. The Catholic Church tried to care for people as best they could. When the government saw this, they thought the Church was taking sides. This put Catholics in danger. Some people told Stanley to leave Guatemala. But Stanley refused. His parishioners were in danger too, and he did not want to leave them.

On July 28, 1981, three men attacked and killed Stanley in his rectory. He died for his faith and the Guatemalan people. We honor Stanley as the first American-born martyr.

Blessed Stanley, you loved the people of Guatemala with all your heart. Help me love and serve the people God has placed in my life. Amen.

August 4
Saint John Vianney
(May 8, 1786–August 4, 1859)

Feast Day: August 4

Patron of confessors and parish priests

John Vianney was born in Lyons, France, in 1786. As a child he took care of his father's sheep. When he was eighteen, he asked his father's permission to become a priest. His father was worried to lose John because he had become a big help on the family farm. But after two years, he agreed to let his son go.

When John was finally able to enter the seminary, studies were difficult. No matter how much he tried, he never did very well. Learning Latin was especially challenging for him. But he still wanted to be a priest, and he thought that was what God wanted, too. When the final examinations came, John had a hard time. He knew the answers, but he had trouble communicating them. He was ordained anyway. His teachers knew that he was a good man and would be a good priest.

John was sent to a little parish called Ars. But he was worried about his people there. They did not care about God or going to church. Many of them led sinful lives. So John fasted and prayed for the people of Ars. He did everything he could to help them turn their lives around and come back to church. Eventually, people started to listen to John. They recognized his holiness and saw the way he lived his life. They respected him, so they wanted to follow his example and become holy, too.

John was very good at giving advice to people. God gave him the power to see into people's minds and know the future. Because of this gift, he converted many sinners and helped people make the right decisions. Pilgrims from all over France began to come to Ars. They wanted to meet John. He would spend more than twelve hours a day hearing confessions. He knew how important it was for people to encounter God's mercy in this sacrament. He served as the priest at Ars for the next forty-two years and died when he was seventy-three.

Saint John Vianney, you struggled a lot in school. But you knew God was with you and you never gave up. Help me trust in God when I have trouble studying. Whether I do well or poorly, never let me forget how much God loves me. Amen.

August 5
Blessed Frédéric Janssoone
(November 19, 1838–August 4, 1916)

Feast Day: August 5

Frédéric was born into a family of wealthy farmers in northern France. He was the youngest of thirteen children and was just nine years old when his father died. He wanted to be a priest, so he started going to school for that. But his mother needed help, so Frédéric went back home to support her. For a while, he worked as a traveling salesman. He liked meeting new people and was good at selling things. When Frédéric was twenty-three, his mother died. This made Frédéric sad, but it also left him free to pursue his dream of becoming a priest. He studied at seminary and became a priest in the Franciscan Order.

For a few years, Frédéric was a military chaplain for soldiers at war. Then in 1876, he was sent to the Holy Land, the place where Jesus was from. While Frédéric was there, he used his skills to help various groups of Christians cooperate with each other in taking care of ancient churches. He brought back the practice of praying the Stations of the Cross in the places where Jesus had actually carried his cross on the streets of Jerusalem. He also built a church in Bethlehem.

Frédéric was then sent to Canada in 1881 to raise money for the Holy Land. His many talents served him well. Now he was connecting with people not to help sell products, but to share the Gospel with them. Frédéric told many interesting stories about the Holy Land. His joyful spirit of self-giving made everyone love him. In 1888, he returned to Canada to stay. He spent the rest of his life there, helping people grow closer to God. Frédéric died of stomach cancer when he was seventy-seven years old.

Blessed Frédéric Janssoone, you used the talents God gave you to make a difference in the world. Help me value the talents God has given me and find ways to use them to help others. Amen.

August 6
Blessed Isidore Bakanja
(c. 1887–August 15, 1909)

Feast Day: August 15

Bakanja was born in the present-day Democratic Republic of the Congo, in Central Africa. His family belonged to the Boangi tribe. They were farmers and fishermen. Bakanja grew up helping his family work the land. When he was about sixteen, he left home to find new work opportunities. At that time, the Congo was under Belgian rule. Many Belgians owned large companies in the Congo. They wanted natives to work for them. Bakanja took a job with a construction company in Bolokwa-Nsimba. It was there that he discovered Christianity.

Bakanja's supervisor was a newly baptized Christian. He introduced Bakanja to the Christian community in Bolokwa-Nsimba. Bakanja was moved by the Gospel message and the faith and love of this community. After about two years, he asked for Baptism. Bakanja took the Christian name Isidore. He also received the brown scapular from the Trappist monks who baptized him. The scapular is worn around the neck as a sign of Mary's blessing and protection. Bakanja treasured this scapular. It reminded him of his new identity in Christ.

In 1908, Bakanja moved to Ikili to work as a domestic servant. There were very few Christians in Ikili. When the workers there saw Bakanja praying, they asked him about his faith. Bakanja eagerly shared the Gospel with them. When Bakanja's manager saw this happening, he was furious. He hated Christianity and its message of social equality. He ordered Bakanja to stop praying. On another occasion, Bakanja's manager saw him wearing his scapular. He ordered Bakanja to remove it. When Bakanja refused, his manager exploded with anger. He had Bakanja severely whipped and left him to die. Eventually, a European inspector found Bakanja. He tried to help him, but it was too late. Bakanja told his caregivers that he forgave his manager and would pray for him from heaven. Bakanja died from his wounds a few months later.

Blessed Isidore Bakanja, you knew that nothing could separate you from Jesus, not even death. Today, help me remember that Jesus is always with me. Amen.

August 7

Saint Mary MacKillop

(January 15, 1842–August 8, 1909)

Feast Day: August 8

Patron of Australia, abuse victims, and the falsely accused

Mary Helen MacKillop was from Australia, the eldest child of Scottish parents. The family had a farm, but they were fairly poor. Mary had to get a job when she was fourteen. Later, she became a teacher.

Mary liked teaching very much. In 1864, with the help of Father Julian Tenison Woods, Mary opened a boarding school for girls in Portland, Victoria (a city in Australia). Two years later, they opened Australia's first Catholic school in a town called Penola. But Mary wanted to do even more. She saw how much children needed a place to learn about their faith and receive a good education. More Catholic schools were necessary. So in 1866, Mary founded the first native Australian religious order. It was called the Sisters of Saint Joseph of the Sacred Heart, or the Josephites.

As a religious sister, Mary chose the name Sister Mary of the Cross. Her work in education expanded rapidly in South Australia and Queensland. Besides schools, Mary and her nuns established orphanages, homes for the elderly, and other institutions. By 1871 she had 130 sisters working in over forty schools.

Despite this success, Mary's life was not easy. She suffered a lot because others misunderstood her and felt jealous of her. Mary was accused of disobedience and misusing her religious congregation's money. This was not true, but Mary was asked to leave the order she had founded. For a time, she was even excommunicated, which means she was cut off from the Church.

Mary was upset, but she trusted that God was still with her. She saw how God was using these events to help her grow closer to him. Eventually, the truth came out and everyone realized they had made a mistake about Mary. She really was a holy woman who was doing good things for God! The excommunication was lifted and Mary was put back in charge of her congregation.

Mary was very happy when her religious order got official approval from Rome. She continued doing good works with great love until her death at age sixty-seven.

Saint Mary MacKillop, you were very passionate about teaching. God used your love of teaching to do much good in the world. Help me develop my own passions and interests so that one day God can use them to build up the kingdom of heaven. Amen.

Saint Dominic

(c. 1170–August 6, 1221)

Feast Day: August 8

Patron of the Dominican Republic, astronomers, and scientists

Dominic was born to the noble Guzmán family in Spain. His family gave him a good example of holiness. Both of his parents and one of his brothers are also the path to becoming saints! When Dominic was seven, he began to go to school. His uncle, a priest, directed his education. After years of study, Dominic became a priest too, following in the footsteps of his older brothers. For a few years, he lived a quiet life of prayer and obedience. But God had amazing plans for Dominic.

It all began when Dominic was on a trip through southern France. He met people who believed in false teachings, or heresies. At that time, the popular heresy was to think that the world was evil and only spiritual things were good. Dominic saw the harm this heresy was doing. He felt sad for the people who believed it. They had forgotten that God loves us and created the world to be good. Dominic wanted to help them return to the true faith. So he founded a group called the Order of Preachers, also known as the Dominicans. The Dominicans preached to people to help them know the truth about God. They prayed hard for those who were affected by heresies, especially by saying the Rosary. Women became Dominicans, too, praying in convents and teaching the people who came to them. Dominic urged the Dominicans to live simple lives and be devoted to prayer and studying the Bible. He was motivated by love of God and neighbor. He wanted his order to be motivated by love, too.

The Dominicans opened centers in France, Spain, and Italy, and then in many other countries. Dominic spent the last few years of his life walking over three thousand miles around Europe to visit his communities and preach to the people. He brought many people back to the Church. Dominic died in 1221 and was declared a saint only thirteen years later. The Dominican Order continued to spread all over the world and is still active today.

Saint Dominic, you wanted everyone to know the truth about God, but you always shared the truth in love. Help me to be kind to others when they are wrong or make mistakes. Help me be humble when I make mistakes, too. Amen.

August 9
Saint Edith Stein
(October 12, 1891–August 9, 1942)

Feast Day: August 9

Patron of Europe, atheists, and loss of parents

Edith was born in Breslau, Germany (modern-day Poland). She grew up in a large Jewish family. Edith was smart and curious about the world. But at age fourteen, she lost her faith in God. She stopped praying and looked in other places, especially books, for the meaning of life. When she was nineteen, she went to college. There she met a famous German philosopher named Edmund Husserl. Edith liked Husserl's ideas about the world and even agreed to work for him after she graduated.

As Edith worked, she met many teachers and philosophers who were Christians. Edith was especially impressed by the Catholic philosopher Max Scheler. These teachers' intelligence and their faith made Edith want to learn more. She started reading the New Testament and writings from the saints. One day, she found a copy of the *Autobiography of Saint Teresa of Ávila* at a friend's house. She started reading and could not put it down. She read all night long. When she finished, she knew she had found the truth she was looking for. Edith decided to become Catholic. She was baptized on New Year's Day in 1922.

As a new Catholic, Edith used her gifts of speaking and writing to teach people about Jesus. She did this for several years. Then in the 1930s, the Nazis rose to power in Germany. They made Edith stop teaching because her family was Jewish. Edith felt lost and afraid. At the same time, she felt a burning desire to pray for God's people. Eventually she realized God was calling her to be a nun. In 1933, Edith entered the Carmelite convent in Cologne, Germany. There she received a new name: Sister Teresa Benedicta of the Cross.

Edith spent the rest of her life praying for peace in the world. Her great wish was for everyone to know and follow Jesus. On August 2, 1942, the Nazis arrested Edith in the convent chapel. She died one week later in a concentration camp, united in spirit with Jesus' death on the cross.

Saint Edith Stein, your search for truth led you to Jesus. He was the answer to all your questions. Help me bring my questions to Jesus, too. Help me learn from the way Jesus lived and died for me. Amen.

Saint Lawrence

(Early Third Century–August 10, 258)

Feast Day: August 10

Patron of cooks, comedians, and firefighters

This famous martyr was one of the seven deacons in charge of giving help to the poor and needy. We know that he died because of an order from Emperor Valerian that all bishops, priests, and deacons should be killed. According to tradition, when the persecution broke out in Rome, the Pope, Saint Sixtus II, was condemned to death. As the Pope was led to his execution, Lawrence followed him, heartbroken that he was losing his spiritual father. He wanted to die for Christ, too. But the Pope told him not to be sad, and that in three days Lawrence would follow him.

After this, the prefect of Rome ordered Lawrence to bring him all the Church's treasure. He was an important government official and a greedy man. He thought there were riches hidden away somewhere and that Lawrence knew where they were. The saint said he would bring the treasure in three days. Then he went through the city and gathered together all the poor and sick people supported by the Church. He showed them to the prefect and said, "This is the Church's treasure." The prefect was furious. In his anger he condemned Lawrence to a slow, cruel death. Saint Ambrose tells the story of how Lawrence was tied on top of an iron grill. Then they roasted him over a slow fire. But even though this was very painful, God gave Lawrence the strength and joy to endure it bravely. Lawrence even joked that they could turn him over because he was done on one side.

Before he died, Lawrence prayed that the city of Rome would be converted to Jesus. He prayed that the Catholic faith would spread to the ends of the Earth. Less than a century later, Christianity had become the official religion of the Roman Empire. From there, it spread all over the world. Emperor Constantine built a church over the place where Lawrence was buried to honor him. Lawrence is one of the saints mentioned in the First Eucharistic Prayer at Mass.

Saint Lawrence, God gave you the grace to be patient and joyful in the most difficult circumstances. Help me to be patient when things are not going my way. Amen.

August 11

Saint Clare of Assisi
(c. July 16, 1194–August 11, 1253)

Feast Day: August 11

Patron of embroidery and needlework, television, and the blind

Clare was born into a rich family in Assisi, Italy. She lived at the time of Saint Francis of Assisi. When she was eighteen, she heard Francis preach. Her heart burned with a great desire to imitate him. Like Francis, she wanted to live a poor, humble life for Jesus. So one evening, she ran away from home. In a little chapel outside Assisi, she gave herself to God.

Francis cut off Clare's hair as a sign of her commitment and offered her a rough brown habit to wear. At first, she stayed with the Benedictine nuns. Her parents tried in every way to make her return home, but Clare would not. Soon, her fifteen-year-old sister Agnes joined her. Agnes also became a saint. Other young women wanted to follow Clare's example and be brides of Jesus. Before long there was a small religious community. They became known as the Poor Clares.

Clare and her nuns lived simple lives of prayer. They wore no shoes and did not eat meat. They lived in a poor house and kept silent most of the time. Yet they were very happy because they were close to Jesus. They were poor outwardly, but they were rich inside because their hearts belonged to God.

Once, an army of rough soldiers came to attack Assisi. They planned to raid the convent first. Although very sick, Clare asked to be carried to the wall. She had the Blessed Sacrament placed right where the soldiers could see it. Then she knelt and begged God to save the nuns. Clare felt God telling her that he would protect them. Then a sudden fright struck the attackers. They ran away as fast as they could.

Clare was the abbess in charge of her convent for almost forty years. For most of those years, she was sick. But she said that she was joyful anyway because she was serving Jesus. Clare was proclaimed a saint just two years after she died.

Saint Clare, you loved Jesus with your whole heart and trusted him with every problem, big and small. Teach me how to trust Jesus the way you did. May my heart grow closer to him every single day. Amen.

August 12
Saint Jane Frances de Chantal
(January 28, 1572–December 13, 1641)

Feast Day: August 12

Patron of parents separated from their children and people who are forgotten

Jane was born in Dijon, France. Her mother died when she was a baby. Her father was a devout man who brought up his children well. As a young woman, Jane married a baron named Christopher de Chantal. Jane and Christopher loved each other very much. God blessed them with four children who survived to adulthood. Jane showed her love for God by loving her husband and children with her whole heart.

Then, suddenly, a great sorrow fell upon that happy home. Christopher was accidentally shot by a friend who had gone hunting with him. When he died, Jane was heartbroken. She did not know what to do next. She began to ask God to send a holy priest into her life to give her guidance.

In the meantime, she prayed and brought up her children in the love of God. She visited the poor and the sick and comforted the dying.

In 1604, Jane met Saint Francis de Sales. She knew this was the holy man God had sent to help her, and the two became good friends. Francis gave Jane advice and helped her with her relationship with God. He also encouraged her to start a religious order called the Congregation of the Visitation. First, however, she had to make sure that her children, although older, were settled. She had other responsibilities and challenges too. But Jane tried to follow God's plan as she saw it, no matter how difficult.

Many women joined the Congregation of the Visitation, and Jane opened up dozens of new convents. She gave guidance to the sisters in her order and to important people who came to her for advice. Jane faced many challenges, especially in her spiritual life. It was not always easy for her to pray, and she seems to have struggled with doubts. But these struggles could not take her out of God's hands. Jane became holy because she continued trusting in God and was always faithful to him. She died at age sixty-nine.

Saint Jane de Chantal, you believed that God held the answers to all your heart's questions. Never let us be afraid of bringing our own questions and doubts to God. Give us the faith to wait patiently and receive his answers when the time is right. Amen.

August 13

Saint Pontian and Saint Hippolytus

(Pontian: Unknown–c. 236; Hippolytus: c. 170–c. 236)

Feast Day: August 13

Hippolytus: Patron of horses and people who work in prisons

Not many details are known about Pontian and Hippolytus' early lives. Pontian became Pope in the year 230. For a few years, things were peaceful. But soon a man named Maximinus became the emperor of Rome. Almost immediately, Maximinus began persecuting Christians. He had Pontian exiled to an island off the coast of Italy called Sardinia.

Pontian knew that he probably would never be allowed to return home. So he stepped down as Pope so that the Church could have a new pope. He did not want his people to be without a leader.

In Sardinia, Pontian was forced to work hard in the mines. He was treated quite harshly. But he offered his sufferings to God for the good of the Church. He also did his best to encourage the other Christians who had been exiled with him. One of them was a man named Hippolytus.

Hippolytus had been a priest and a scholar in the church of Rome. He wrote many excellent works of theology and was a great teacher. But Hippolytus had extreme views about certain things. He became frustrated with Saint Zephyrinus, a pope who was martyred in the year 217. He felt that Zephyrinus had not been quick enough to stop people who were teaching errors. Hippolytus did not like the next pope, Saint Callistus I, either. He decided to break ties with the Church and become a false pope.

When Maximinus' persecution began, Hippolytus was arrested and sent to Sardinia. It was there that God worked a miracle. Hippolytus began talking with Pontian. Although they had been enemies before, Hippolytus was starting to see the mistake he had made. He was touched by Pontian's humility and love for God. He was sorry that he had led people astray and not listened to the true popes. So Hippolytus asked Pontian for forgiveness. Pontian received Hippolytus back into the Church with great joy.

In the end, both Pontian and Hippolytus became martyrs for the faith, united in their love for Jesus.

Saints Pontian and Hippolytus, you worked through your differences and reconciled with each other. This brought you peace and joy in dark times. Give me the courage to apologize when I hurt someone or make a mistake. Teach me how to accept the apologies of others with a loving heart. Amen.

August 14

Saint Maximilian Kolbe

(January 7, 1894–August 14, 1941)

Feast Day: August 14

Patron of addicts, journalists, prisoners

Raymond Kolbe was born in Poland. He joined the Franciscan Order as a teenager and took the name Maximilian. Maximilian loved his vocation, and he especially loved the Blessed Mother. He added the name Mary to his religious name when he pronounced his solemn vows in 1914. He also became a priest.

Maximilian was convinced that the people of the modern world needed Mary to guide and protect them. He used the press to make Mary more widely known. He and his fellow Franciscans published newsletters that soon went to readers around the world. He also built a large center in Poland called the City of Mary Immaculate. By 1938, eight hundred Franciscans lived there. They worked to make the love of Jesus and Mary known. Maximilian then started a City of Mary Immaculate in Nagasaki, Japan, and another in India.

Meanwhile in Germany, the Nazi political party took over. They invaded Poland in 1939 and tried to stop the wonderful work going on in the Polish City of Mary Immaculate. But for a few years, the Franciscans, led by Maximilian, continued their publications. They also took in thousands of refugees, many of whom were Jewish. Then in 1941, the Nazis arrested Maximilian. They sentenced him to hard manual labor at a camp in Auschwitz.

In Auschwitz, Maximilian did everything he could to help his fellow prisoners. He would pray with them and say the Mass in secret. But after two months, a prisoner escaped. The Nazis made the rest of the prisoners pay. They made them stand in a line and picked ten men randomly to be killed. One chosen prisoner had a family. He begged to be spared for the sake of his children. Maximilian, who had not been picked, felt deeply moved to help that suffering prisoner. He volunteered to die in the man's place.

Maximilian and the other unlucky prisoners were sentenced to a slow, painful death. But even then, Maximilian did not lose his faith. He prayed constantly, comforting his companions until the end. He knew that a beautiful heaven awaited them.

Saint Maximilian Kolbe, you learned how to be brave and trust in God from the Blessed Mother. Help us to love Mary and follow her example like you did. Whenever we feel scared or alone, remind us to pray a Hail Mary. Amen.

The Assumption of the Blessed Virgin Mary

Feast Day: August 15

Mary is very special because she was chosen to be Jesus' mother, the Mother of God. Throughout her whole life, Mary did God's will. She lovingly raised Jesus until he was an adult. Then, when Jesus started preaching and performing miracles, Mary was still with him at important moments in his life. She was there for his first public miracle at the wedding feast in Cana. She was also there at the foot of the cross when he died.

After Jesus rose from the dead and ascended into heaven, Mary stayed with his disciples. She prayed with them and guided them. She was at Pentecost when God sent the Holy Spirit and the Church began. She helped the apostles during the first years of the Church and told them stories about when Jesus was a child. During all this time, Mary stayed close to God and Jesus through prayer. She longed to be reunited with her Son, who was already in heaven.

At the end of Mary's life, an amazing thing happened. God did not just bring her soul up to heaven—he brought her body, too! We call this the assumption, when Mary was "assumed" into heaven, body and soul. This was a special privilege that God gave Mary because she was the mother of Jesus. Now Mary is in heaven with Jesus. She is the Queen of Heaven and Earth. She is the Mother of Jesus' Church, and she still watches over us today. Every time Mary asks Jesus to give us graces, he listens to her request.

But Mary is not the only one who will get to have a body in heaven. Jesus rose from the dead so that one day we could all be resurrected from the dead. Like the bodies of Jesus and Mary, our resurrected bodies will be perfect. We will be happy with God forever in heaven with both our souls and our bodies.

Mary showed us the way. Her assumption into heaven helps us to trust in God's promise that someday everyone's bodies will be resurrected.

Mary, you are already in heaven, body and soul. You know how precious our bodies are to God. They should be precious to us, too. Help us to take care of our bodies and to treat them with respect. And one day, may we come join you in heaven! Amen.

August 16
Saint Stephen of Hungary
(c. 975–August 15, 1038)

Feast Day: August 16

Patron of Hungary

Stephen was born to a noble family in Hungary. His father was the duke of Hungary. At that time, Christianity was just being brought to the country. Stephen was about ten years old when he first learned about Jesus. He and his family became Christian, and so did many of the other nobles. However, much of the rest of the country still followed the old religions.

Stephen was in his twenties when he became the ruler of Hungary. He made it his goal to help everyone in the country become Christian. God blessed Stephen's efforts, and the Church became strong in Hungary. One reason for Stephen's amazing success was his devotion to Mary. He placed his whole kingdom under the Blessed Mother's protection. He also built a magnificent church in her honor. Pope Sylvester II wanted to thank Stephen for everything he had done for the Church, so he sent a beautiful king's crown to Stephen. This became known as Saint Stephen's Crown. It is still a national treasure in Hungary today.

Stephen was a strong, fearless ruler. But he was also gentle and kind to the poor. He tried to avoid war as much as he could. He loved to give gifts of money to beggars without letting them know who he was. One legend says that he was giving these gifts in disguise one day when a crowd of rough beggars knocked him down. They struck him and stole his money pouch. They never could have imagined they were bullying their king. And they never found out from him. Stephen took the insult quietly and humbly. He prayed for those beggars and decided to give more money than ever to the poor. This was because he knew how much Jesus loved the poor.

Stephen was the king of Hungary for many years, until his death in 1048.

Saint Stephen, you always tried to lead your country according to God's will. You know that political leaders have to make many difficult decisions. Please help the leaders of our country listen to God's voice. Guide them to do what is best for their people. Amen.

Blessed Marie-Élisabeth Turgeon

(February 7, 1840–August 17, 1881)

Feast Day: August 17

Élisabeth was born into a large family in Quebec, Canada. When she was fifteen, her father died. Élisabeth wanted to go to school to become a teacher, but for the next five years, she stayed home to help her mother raise the younger children. When she was twenty, she was able to enroll in school to obtain her teaching degree. She began to teach at a school not far from her family home. Élisabeth's health was always frail and it would cause problems throughout her life. After a few years, she could not continue teaching because of health problems. When she recovered, she began to teach again, but then the same thing happened. So Élisabeth prayed to Saint Anne, asking for healing. She promised that if she was healed, she would teach for free. Her health did get better, so she carried out her promise and did not charge her students any money.

Around that time, Father John Langevin invited her to join a community of sisters he was starting, called the Sisters of the Little Schools. After much prayer and reflection, Élisabeth entered the community. She helped train new teachers for the parish schools. Father Langevin soon became a bishop. After a few years, with the bishop's approval and help, Élisabeth started a new community. It was called the Sisters of Our Lady of the Rosary.

More women joined and the community grew. But Élisabeth started to have health problems again. She still continued to carry out her teaching work as best she could. She founded schools in remote, rural areas so that the children there could have a good education. She also wrote textbooks full of clever sayings that were used in the schools. And she provided guidance for the other sisters in her community. But by the summer of 1881 her health had gotten so bad that she was at the point of death. She died on August 17, two days after the feast of Our Lady's Assumption into heaven.

Blessed Élisabeth, you desired to teach so that the light of faith would reach many people. Pray for us, that with our lives and our words, we too may help others to know and love Jesus. Amen.

August 18
Saint Alberto Hurtado Cruchaga
(January 22, 1901–August 18, 1952)

Feast Day: August 18

Patron of homeless children, social workers, and the poor

Alberto was born into a wealthy family in Chile. But after his father died when Alberto was four, his family fell on hard times. They lost their house and had to live with various relatives. Alberto earned a scholarship to a good school run by the Jesuits. He obtained a law degree. But his heart was longing for something more. He entered the Jesuits in 1923 and was ordained a priest ten years later.

His superiors sent him to study in Spain and then Belgium. When he returned to Chile, he taught at the university. In 1940 he became active in the Catholic Action youth movement. This was a group for people who wanted to live their Catholic faith more intentionally and share it with others. He was made its national director the next year. The needs of the poor moved him, especially homeless children. He wanted to do something for them. A few years later while giving a retreat, he asked for help for a special project he had in mind. It was called El Hogar de Cristo, or the Home of Christ. Its goal was to provide shelter for the homeless. He opened the first house for children, and later one for women and another for men. The movement spread quickly and soon there were many homes throughout Chile.

Alberto also wrote books and pamphlets about social justice. He even started a magazine. His big heart wanted to help everyone in need. Alberto made sure that he helped people not only with their material needs, but with their spiritual needs as well. He brought the love of Christ to everyone and preached the Gospel fervently. He died of pancreatic cancer when he was fifty-one years old.

Saint Alberto, pray for us that we might be more aware of the needs of the people around us. When we can lend a helping hand, help us to do so with a warm and generous heart like you always did. Amen.

August 19
Saint John Eudes
(November 14, 1601–August 19, 1680)

Feast Day: August 19

Patron of missionaries

John Eudes was born in Normandy, France. He was the oldest son of a farmer. Even as a child, he tried to copy the example of Jesus in the way he treated his family, friends, and neighbors. One story says that when John was nine, another boy slapped his face. John felt himself becoming angry. Then he remembered how Jesus says we should turn the other cheek. So he did, forgiving the other boy instead of starting a fight.

John's parents wanted him to get married and have a family. He gently but firmly convinced them that he was called to be a priest instead. He decided to join the Congregation of the Oratory. There, he studied for the priesthood and was ordained in 1625. But right after John became a priest, the plague hit Normandy. It brought terrible suffering and death. John volunteered to help the sick, caring for both their souls and bodies. He knew that he might catch the disease himself, but he was willing to take the risk to minister to those in need.

Once the disaster had passed, John became a popular preacher. He traveled to many parishes, giving sermons to help people grow closer to God. One of John's favorite topics to preach about was the Sacred Heart of Jesus and the Holy Heart of Mary. These devotions remind us of how much Jesus and Mary love us and how we can always turn to them when we need help. John is also responsible for establishing important religious congregations like the Sisters of Our Lady of Charity and the Congregation of Jesus and Mary for priests. This congregation is dedicated to training young men to become good parish priests.

Eventually, John became sick after he preached an outdoor mission in very cold weather. He never fully recovered. John was seventy-eight years old when he died.

Saint John Eudes, you always prayed to the Sacred Hearts of Jesus and Mary. Help me to know how much Jesus and Mary love me. May my heart become more and more like theirs every day! Amen.

August 20
Saint Bernard of Clairvaux
(1090–August 20, 1153)

Feast Day: August 20

Patron of beekeepers, climbers, and the Cistercian Order

Bernard was born to a noble family in Dijon, France. He and his six brothers and one sister received an excellent education. When Bernard was a teenager, his mother died. He took it very hard. He might have let sadness get the best of him had it not been for his lively sister, Humbeline. She cheered him up and soon Bernard became a very popular man. He was handsome and intelligent, full of fun and good humor. People enjoyed being with him.

One day, Bernard shocked his friends by telling them he was going to join the strict Cistercian Order and become a monk. They tried to make him give up the idea. But, in the end, it was Bernard who convinced his brothers, uncle, and twenty-six friends to join him at the Cistercian monastery.

Bernard became a very good monk. He loved living a life totally dedicated to prayer and God. After three years, he was sent to start a new Cistercian monastery in Clairvaux. Bernard was the abbot there for the rest of his life.

Although he would have liked to stay working and praying in his monastery, Bernard was called out sometimes for special assignments. He preached, made peace between rulers, and advised popes. He also wrote beautiful spiritual books. He became one of the most influential men of his time. Yet Bernard did not care about becoming famous. His great desire was to be a good monk and to be close to God.

Bernard had a great devotion to the Blessed Mother. It is said that he often greeted her with a "Hail Mary" when he passed her statue. Then one day, the Blessed Mother apparently greeted him back! In this way, Mary showed how much Bernard's love and devotion pleased her.

Bernard was around sixty-three years old when he died. He was named a doctor of the Church because of his important writings about theology and the faith.

Saint Bernard, people liked to spend time with you, but you were not interested in popularity. Instead, you used your influence to inspire your friends and family to follow God more closely. Teach me not to worry about becoming popular. Help me to be a good influence on my friends. Amen.

August 21
Saint Pius X
(June 2, 1835–August 20, 1914)

Feast Day: August 21

Patron of catechists, first communicants, and pilgrims

Joseph Sarto was the son of a mailman in Riese, Italy. When Joseph felt that God wanted him to be a priest, he had to make many sacrifices for his education. He even walked miles to school barefoot to save his one good pair of shoes. But he did not mind. He was excited to be doing something for God with his life.

After Joseph was ordained a priest, he served in poor parishes for several years, taking care of the people there. His parishioners loved him. He used to give away everything he had to help them, even his own food and clothing! This did not change when Joseph became a bishop and a cardinal. He still gave away what he owned to the poor, keeping nothing for himself.

When Pope Leo XIII died in 1903, Joseph was chosen to be the new pope. He took the name Pius X. He became known as the Pope who loved the Holy Eucharist. Pius encouraged everyone to receive Jesus in Communion as often as they could. He made a law that allowed young children to receive the Eucharist too. Before that time, boys and girls had to wait many years before they could receive their first Communion. Pius also encouraged religious instruction. He believed in and loved our Catholic faith. He wanted every Catholic to be able to know about it. He encouraged priests and religion teachers to help everyone learn about their faith.

Pius loved the members of the Church as his own children and cared for them like a father. When the terrible World War I broke out, he suffered greatly. Pius knew that so many people would be killed. He said he would give up his own life if that could save his people from the war. Not long after, Pius died. He was seventy-nine years old.

Saint Pius X, you shared everything with the poor. Help me to have a generous heart like you did. Whether it is extra clothes, food, toys, or money, remind me to share what I have with the needy. Amen.

August 22
Blessed Victoria Rasoamanarivo
(1848–August 21, 1894)

Feast Day: August 21

Patron of Madagascar, lay leaders, and troubled marriages

Victoria was a princess of the royal family in Madagascar, an island off the coast of Africa. Her uncle was in charge of her schooling. When she was thirteen, she attended a school run by the Sisters of Saint Joseph of Cluny. She became interested in the Catholic faith and asked the sisters many questions about God. She would often ask, "Is God good?" The sisters always told her yes, God is good. Her uncle was upset when she told him she wanted to be baptized. But Victoria held firm. Eventually he agreed and she was baptized at age fifteen.

As a Catholic, Victoria thought of becoming a nun. But she agreed to marriage because of her family position. Her husband, a man named Radriaka, was chosen for her by her uncle. It was a bad choice. Radriaka often drank too much and was unfaithful to Victoria. She suffered a lot in her marriage. But she loved her husband and was always faithful. After many years, he softened and asked for Baptism on his deathbed.

In the meantime, Victoria undertook many charitable works. She started Catholic Action, a group devoted to helping the poor and bringing them the Christian faith. She tended the sick, especially lepers. She also visited prisoners. In 1883 a war broke out between the French and the local government. The queen of Madagascar expelled all the French people, including missionaries. Victoria then became an important leader of the Catholics. The queen had locked all the churches. But one Sunday, Victoria and a group of people marched up to the doors of their cathedral. Soldiers were guarding it but Victoria demanded that the group be let in. The soldiers did not want to oppose her. So the people were allowed in to pray.

For three years, there were no priests in Madagascar. But Victoria helped the Catholics to keep their faith by gathering together for prayer. When the priests returned three years later, they found about twenty-one thousand Catholics in Madagascar who had remained faithful. Victoria died of an illness when she was forty-six years old.

Blessed Victoria, you faced many trials in life but you did not feel sorry for yourself. When some difficulty arises in my life, help me to respond with faith like you did. Amen.

August 23

Saint Rose of Lima

(April 20, 1586–August 24, 1617)

Feast Day: August 23

Patron of Latin and South America, the Philippines, and gardeners

Rose was born in Lima, Peru. Her real name was Isabel, but she was such a beautiful baby that she was called Rose. As Rose grew older, she became more and more beautiful. One day her mother put a wreath of flowers on her head to show off her loveliness to friends. But Rose was not impressed. She did not think she was special because of her looks. She realized that beauty is a gift from God. She also did not want men trying to marry her because of her beauty. She had already decided that she wanted to belong only to Jesus.

Rose humbly obeyed her parents, except when they tried to get her to marry. That she would not do. She prayed that her parents would be more accepting of her life with Jesus. Finally, when Rose was twenty, they agreed to let her become a Third Order Dominican. This meant that Rose followed a Dominican spirituality and prayed often, but she continued living at home.

Rose spent much of her time in prayer. She sewed lace and grew flowers to sell. The money helped support her family and the poor. She also took care of those who were sick and needed help. Rose grew much closer to Jesus. But there were times when she had to suffer terrible loneliness and sadness. During those times, God seemed far away. Yet she cheerfully offered all these troubles to him. She kept praying for her trust to grow stronger.

Rose was only thirty-one when she got sick and died. But her heart was full of love for God, even during her painful illness. Rose's funeral was packed with people from Lima. They all wanted to say goodbye to their beloved saint.

Saint Rose, you did not spend much time worrying about what you looked like. Instead, you wanted your soul to be beautiful for Jesus. Help me to not judge people based on their physical appearances. Teach me to focus on what is really important: loving God and others. Amen.

August 24
Saint Bartholomew .
(Unknown–c. 51)

Feast Day: August 24

Patron of Armenia, leather workers, and against skin disease

Bartholomew was one of the first followers of Jesus. His other name was Nathaniel. He came from Cana in Galilee. He became a disciple of Jesus when his friend, Saint Philip, invited him to come and meet the Lord. When Jesus saw Nathaniel approaching, he said, "Here is truly an Israelite in whom there is no deceit!" (Jn 1:47). Jesus meant that Nathaniel was an honest, sincere man who would never deceive anyone. His one desire was to know the truth.

Nathaniel was very surprised to hear those words from Jesus, since he had never met Jesus before. "Where did you get to know me?" he asked. Jesus answered, "I saw you under the fig tree before Philip called you" (Jn 1:48). How did Jesus know what Nathaniel had been doing before they had met each other? Some say that Nathaniel had been praying as he sat under the fig tree. Nathaniel realized that Jesus had read his heart as he prayed. Immediately, he started to believe in Jesus and exclaimed, "You are the Son of God! You are the King of Israel!" (Jn 1:49).

After that, Nathaniel—or Bartholomew, as he was also called—became one of Jesus' faithful apostles. He traveled with Jesus while Jesus preached and performed miracles. Once Jesus had risen from the dead and ascended into heaven, Bartholomew spent the rest of his life telling others about Jesus. According to tradition, he went all over the world, to places like Ethiopia, India, and modern-day Iran.

He preached the Gospel to the people there, even at the risk of his own life. Eventually Bartholomew died for the faith. He became a martyr while he was preaching in Armenia.

Saint Bartholomew, Jesus praised you for your honesty. You then dedicated your whole life to spreading the truth that he shared with you. Help me to be honest with others. Whether it is in big matters or small ones, may I always tell the truth in a loving way. Amen.

August 25

Saint Louis of France
(April 25, 1214–August 25, 1270)

Feast Day: August 25

Patron of France, builders, and science

Louis' father was King Louis VIII of France. His mother was Queen Blanche. She was a faithful Catholic and brought Louis up to cherish his faith. Louis received the best education and learned skills like hunting and horseback riding. When he was twelve, his father died and Louis became the king. But Queen Blanche made most of the decisions until he was older.

When Louis was twenty years old, he married Margaret, the daughter of a count. They loved each other very much. They had eleven children. Louis was a good husband and father. And as long as his mother, Queen Blanche, lived, he showed her full respect.

Louis became a remarkable ruler. He was generous and fair. He ruled his people with wisdom, love, and guidance from his faith. He knew how to settle arguments and disputes. He listened to the poor and paid attention to everybody, not just the rich and influential. But as busy as he was, Louis always made time for God. He went to daily Mass and prayed often. He was a Third Order Franciscan and lived a simple lifestyle in the spirit of Saint Francis of Assisi. He also supported Catholic education and built monasteries.

Louis was not just concerned for his own people in France. He also believed it was important to help the Christians in the Holy Land, the place where Jesus was from. The Christians there were being persecuted for their faith. Louis wanted to be a part of the Crusades, which were campaigns to make Christianity the main religion of the Holy Land. Twice, he led an army against the Turks. The first time, he was taken prisoner in Egypt. He was eventually freed and returned to France to take care of his kingdom. Yet as soon as he could, Louis set out with his men once more.

Before much fighting had taken place, Louis became very ill. He spent his final hours preparing his son, Philip, to be the new king. He gave Philip advice about how to be a good ruler and a good Christian. Louis died at peace, eager to see God in heaven.

Saint Louis, family was very important to you. Even with all your responsibilities, you tried hard to be a good son and a good father. Help us to be good sons and daughters, good brothers and sisters. May we love our family members as much as Jesus loves them. Amen.

August 26
Saint Mariam Baouardy
(January 5, 1846–August 26, 1878)

Feast Day: August 26

Patron of peace in the Near and Middle East

Mariam was born to a devout family in Galilee in the Holy Land. Her parents had twelve boys who all died in infancy. They then made a pilgrimage to Bethlehem to pray that they would have a girl. Mariam was born shortly after in answer to their prayers. Two years later they had another son, Paul, who survived. But when Mariam was three years old, both of her parents died.

Left as an orphan, Mariam was taken in by an uncle. They moved to Alexandria in Egypt when she was eight years old. When she was older, her uncle arranged a marriage for her. That was the custom at the time. But Mariam did not want to get married because she wanted to become a nun. She protested and refused to marry. Her uncle became very angry with her and made her become a servant in the household. She was treated very badly. When she was able to leave, she found work with a kind family as a domestic servant.

Mariam still had the dream of becoming a nun. She entered the Sisters of Saint Joseph in France. But she was starting to have some mystical experiences. The sisters thought she would be better suited to a Carmelite monastery, so they sent her there. She took the name Sister Mary of Jesus Crucified, and in 1871 she made her profession of vows. She continued to have many special mystical graces. These included the stigmata, which were the wounds of

Jesus on the cross appearing on her hands and feet. They caused her pain, but she did not complain because they helped her feel united to Jesus.

Mariam was sent to India to help start a new monastery for the Carmelites there. She stayed two years and then went back to the Holy Land. She helped to establish two more Carmelite monasteries, one in Bethlehem and one in Nazareth. One day she fell and had a bad accident that caused a serious wound. Mariam died shortly after, offering her life for the Church in union with Jesus.

Saint Mariam, you had a difficult road to travel before you could follow your vocation as a nun. Pray for those whom God is calling to the religious life. Help them to follow his call and serve him with joy. Amen.

August 27

Saint Monica

(c. 332–387)

Feast Day: August 27

Patron of alcoholics, mothers, and patience

Monica was born in Tagaste, which is in modern-day Algeria. She was brought up as a good Christian. This was a great help to her when she married Patricius, a Roman official. Patricius admired his wife, but he did not like her religion. He made Monica suffer because of his bad temper, and he would not let her baptize their children. Monica loved her husband as best she could, but she would not stop practicing her faith. For years, she prayed for her husband's conversion. Slowly, Patricius was won over by Monica's example and love. He was finally baptized on his deathbed in 372.

Monica's joy over the holy way in which her husband had died soon changed to great sorrow. She found out that her son Augustine was living a bad, selfish life. This brilliant young man had turned to a false religion and to immoral habits. Monica prayed and cried for her son. She begged priests to talk to him. Augustine was brilliant, yet very stubborn. He did not want to give up his sinful life. But Monica would not give up either. When Augustine went to Rome without her, she followed him. At Rome, she learned he had become a teacher in Milan. So Monica went to Milan. And in all that time, she never stopped praying for him.

After several years, God answered Monica's prayers in great abundance. Augustine finally saw the truth of Christianity and changed his life around. Not only did Augustine become a good Christian, as she had prayed. He also became a priest, a bishop, a great writer, and a famous saint. Monica's patience and love for her son had finally paid off.

Monica and Augustine became very close after that. But Monica's health was failing. Augustine spent much time at her bedside. Together, they had a mystical prayer experience of God's love. After this, Monica had a great desire to go to heaven and be with God. Augustine was with Monica when she died in Ostia, outside of Rome.

Saint Monica, you did not become discouraged when your prayers were not answered right away. Instead, you trusted in God and kept praying. Never let me give up on my prayers. May I truly believe that God always hears me and will answer me with great love and generosity. Amen.

August 28

Saint Augustine

(November 13, 354–August 28, 430)

Feast Day: August 28

Patron of brewers, printers, and theologians

Augustine was born in northern Africa, in the city of Tagaste. His mother, Saint Monica, tried to teach him about Christianity and give him a good upbringing. He received a good education and was very intelligent. But as Augustine grew older, he became proud and immoral. All he cared about was seeking pleasure and fame.

That kind of lifestyle did not keep Augustine satisfied for long. He started looking for deeper meaning in his life. At first, he got caught up in a false religion. He followed it for years until he discovered that it could not answer all his questions. Then he moved on to other philosophies. But none of them were quite right. Augustine's heart was still restless.

At that time, Augustine was living in the city of Milan. He got to know the bishop of Milan, Saint Ambrose. Augustine would listen to Ambrose's sermons and ask him questions. Augustine's mother, Monica, also had a good influence on him. Every day, she prayed for his conversion. With their help, Augustine realized that Christianity was the true religion that could satisfy his heart and lead him to God. Still, it was difficult for him to convert to Christianity. He was attached to his sinful habits and did not think he was strong enough to give them up. Then he had an experience in prayer that made him feel called to follow Jesus with all his heart.

After that, Augustine began a new life. He trusted that God would give him the strength he needed to live as a good Christian. And God did. Augustine was baptized in 387. Later, he was ordained a priest and the bishop of Hippo, a city in modern-day Algeria. He put his intelligence at the service of God by preaching and writing many brilliant books. He overcame false teachings, lived simply, and supported the poor. Augustine also prayed with great love right up until his death at age seventy-five. His heart had finally found its rest in God.

Saint Augustine, your life is proof that it is never too late to start loving God and making good decisions. When I make a mistake, help me to admit that I was wrong and seek forgiveness. Remind me that no matter what happens, I can always come back to God. Amen.

August 29
Saint Euphrasia Eluvathingal
(October 17, 1877–August 29, 1952)

Feast Day: August 30

Rosa Euphrasia was born in Kerala, India. She was one of five children. The family belonged to the Syro-Malabar Rite of the Catholic Church. Even from her childhood, Rosa had a desire to give herself totally to Jesus. When she was a little older, she told her parents that she wanted to become a nun. She wanted to enter the Sisters of the Mother of

Carmel. Her father was very much opposed to this. But she kept on praying, and after a while, he agreed to let her join the convent.

Rosa was very happy to become a Carmelite. She was given the name Sister Euphrasia of the Sacred Heart of Jesus. Soon after entering the community, Rosa suffered from frequent poor health. When she was a novice, her superiors almost sent her back home for health reasons. But then she had a vision of the Holy Family and was miraculously cured.

Sister Euphrasia made her vows, and in 1904 she was asked to become the novice mistress. This meant that she would guide the young sisters, called novices, and teach them all about Carmelite life. They loved her because she was very kind and guided them well. In 1913 Sister Euphrasia was asked to become the superior of one of the convents. She felt she was not suitable for this office. But she accepted it and trusted in God to help her. She even got a statue of the Sacred Heart of Jesus and enthroned it as if Jesus were the superior.

Sister Euphrasia's whole life was marked by prayer. The local people called her "the Praying Mother." She would spend long hours of prayer before Jesus in the Blessed Sacrament. She also had a great devotion to Mary, our Blessed Mother. In her prayers she remembered all the people of the world. She especially asked God to help the Church in its needs.

Saint Euphrasia, you devoted your life to prayer. Help us to remember to spend some time each day in prayer. Help us also to pray for the needs of the Church and the whole world. Amen.

August 30
Saint Jeanne Jugan
(October 25, 1792–August 29, 1879)

Feast Day: August 30

Patron of the poor, the elderly, and caretakers of the elderly

Jeanne's life was marked by great humility and love for the poor. She was born in Brittany, France, and had seven siblings. She lived during difficult times. The Church was being persecuted, but Jeanne's mother still made sure her children were taught the Catholic faith. Her father was a fisherman who died at sea when Jeanne was about four years old. Jeanne grew up working hard, helping with jobs at home. She was also a shepherdess and later worked as a maid to help her family. A good man asked her to marry him, but she said no because she felt God was calling her to something else.

Jeanne worked in a hospital for some time. Then, one day, she came across an elderly woman who was blind and sick. The woman had no one to help her. Jeanne brought her home and cared for her. She even slept in the attic, giving the old woman her own room. Jeanne fell in love with this way of life that God was calling her to. Slowly, more elderly poor people found their way to Jeanne's house. Other people started to help Jeanne care for them. Eventually she founded a new religious congregation called the Little Sisters of the Poor. Jeanne took the name Sister Mary of the Cross.

Although she was the one who started the Little Sisters, the priest in charge forced Jeanne to be on the sidelines. He sent her out begging for food with the other sisters and eventually forced her to retire. For the next twenty-seven years, no one knew she was the original founder. It was only later that her true place as the founder was made known. Through all this, Jeanne showed great humility, wanting only to serve God in the poor. She did not care about earthly fame. Today, the Little Sisters have spread all over the world, continuing Jeanne's work.

Saint Jeanne Jugan, you showed us how to care for others and practiced deep humility. Pray for me that I might also see the image of Christ in each person I meet and treat them like I would treat Jesus. Amen.

August 31
Saint Aidan of Lindisfarne
(c. 590–August 31, 651)

Feast Day: August 31
Patron of firefighters

Aidan was born in Ireland. As a young man, he decided to become a monk and dedicate his life to God. He went to live at the great monastery of Iona, an island off the coast of Scotland.

At that time, there were still parts of England that Christianity had not reached. One of these areas was Northumbria, in northern England. In 634, Saint Oswald became the king of Northumbria. He asked the monastery at Iona to send missionaries to preach to his people. The first missionary to go had little success. He soon came back complaining that the English were rude, stubborn, and wild. Aidan thought he was being too harsh. When the monks got together to talk about the situation, Aidan reminded them of the way Saint Paul had taught people: first, easy teachings are given. Then, when the people have grown stronger on the word of God, they are able to receive the harder teachings.

As soon as the monks heard Aidan's wise words, they decided he should be the one to go to Northumbria. Aidan took on this missionary assignment with humility and a spirit of prayer. He traveled all over northern England, always on foot. He began by preaching. King Oswald himself translated Aidan's sermons into English until Aidan learned the language better. But Aidan did not only preach with words. He also showed people who Jesus was by his actions, helping those in need. Because of Aidan's teachings and example, many English converted.

Aidan built a large church and monastery on the island of Lindisfarne, off the northeastern coast of England. He was chosen to be the bishop of Lindisfarne and the surrounding area. Lindisfarne became an important center for the Church in England for many centuries. So many saints later came from there that Lindisfarne became known as the Holy Island.

After many years of lovingly serving the English people, Aidan died when he was around sixty.

Saint Aidan, you show us that the witness of a joyful, kind person is a powerful influence on others. Help us to see the good in people and to treat them the way we want to be treated. Amen.

September 1

Saint Giles

(c. 650–c. 710)

Feast Day: September 1

Patron of horses, people who are afraid of the night, and those who are disabled

Giles was one of the most popular saints in the Middle Ages, but little is known about his life except the traditions that have been handed down about him. Giles was born in Athens, Greece. When his parents died, he inherited a large fortune. He used that money to help the poor. He had a reputation for being a holy man and God worked many miracles through him. Because of this, the people of Athens greatly admired him. But Giles did not want this praise and fame at all. He wanted to lead a hidden life where he could serve God quietly. So Giles sailed to France and went to live alone in a dark forest.

He made his home in a rough cave that was hidden behind a thick thorn bush. He was happy to spend his days praying without any distractions. He found roots and plants to eat and became friends with a deer that would come to his cave. But one day, the king and his men were hunting in the woods. They chased the deer, but it escaped by running into Giles' cave. One of the men shot an arrow into the thorn bush, hoping to hit the deer. When they forced their way in, they were surprised to see that Giles was there. The arrow had accidentally hit his leg. The men wanted to know who Giles was, so he told them the story of his life. When they heard it, they asked his forgiveness. Then the king sent his doctors to take care of Giles.

Although Giles begged to be left alone, the king respected him so much that he often came to visit. Other people heard about Giles and found the cave, too, asking for his advice and prayers. Eventually the king built a large monastery and put Giles in charge as the first abbot. Many people came there to dedicate their lives to God. The monastery became so famous that a whole town grew up around it. When the saint died, his grave at the monastery became a great pilgrimage site.

Saint Giles, you wanted to live a quiet life, but God had other plans for you. Help us pay attention to how God might be working in our lives when things do not go the way we plan. Amen.

September 2

Blessed Jean du Lau and the September Martyrs of the French Revolution

(died September 2 and 3, 1792)

Feast Day: September 2

Jean du Lau was the archbishop of Arles, France. He and his 190 companions were martyrs from the French

Revolution. In 1790, a new constitution that was against the Church was created in France. The people were being forced to sign their agreement with an oath. If they did not, they were punished. At first, that just meant being put in prison. But by 1792, things were getting out of control. People were being killed if they did not support the constitution.

Many brave bishops, priests, religious, and laypeople would not sign the oath supporting the French constitution. They knew they would be betraying God and his Church if they did. The Pope told them that they were right to resist. It was a sad time for the people of France.

Priests and religious were being held captive in monasteries and convents that had been turned into prisons. They used the time in prison for prayer, and God strengthened them for what was coming. On September 2, 1792, a huge crowd rioted and broke into one of these monasteries. The mob approached the priests and told them to sign the oath. Each of them refused and was killed.

The rioters then went to the Carmelite church. Jean and other bishops and priests were being held there. All refused to take the oath and were murdered. One of the martyrs was André Grasset. He had been born in Montreal, Canada. But his family returned to France and he became a priest there. He knew that he was risking his life by remaining loyal to the Church. But when the violent crowd asked him to sign the oath, he told them that his conscience would not allow him to. He was the first person born in Canada to be declared a blessed.

The next day, the same mob went to the Lazarist seminary. It was a temporary prison for ninety priests and religious. Only four survived. By the end of the French Revolution, 1,500 Catholics had been killed. They would not compromise their faithfulness to God and the Church, even at the cost of their lives.

Blessed Jean du Lau and the September martyrs, you went against the crowd even though it was scary, because you loved God and the Church so much. Help me to be brave when I have to stand up for what I know is right. Amen.

September 3
Saint Gregory the Great
(c. 540–March 12, 604)

Feast Day: September 3

Patron of the West Indies, musicians, and singers

Gregory was born to a prestigious family in Rome. He was raised as a Christian—his mother and a few other relatives are also saints. Gregory was very smart and talented. While he was still young, he became one of the most important government officials in Rome. He wanted to serve others, but he also wanted to devote more of his time to God. So when he was thirty-four years old, Gregory turned his large house into a monastery. He lived for several years as a good and holy monk. Then the Pope made him a deacon and gave him important jobs to do. When the Pope died, Gregory was chosen to take his place. He was so holy and wise that everyone knew he would be a good pope. But Gregory did not want that honor at all. It was very hard for him to accept the task. But once he felt it was God's will, he poured his whole heart into being a good pope.

For fourteen years he served the Church as Pope. Even though his health was poor, Gregory was one of the greatest popes the Church has ever had. He navigated the Church through complex political situations. He wrote many books and was a wonderful preacher. He cared for people all over the world and helped other countries become more open to Christianity. He was also sensitive to injustice and worked hard to get rid of corruption in the Church. Gregory especially loved the poor and outcasts. Every day he used to feed them a good dinner. In fact, he considered himself the servant of all. He was the first pope to use the title "servant of the servants of God," a title our popes today still use.

Gregory's last years were filled with great sufferings, yet he continued working for his beloved Church until the very end of his life.

Saint Gregory the Great, you did not want to be the pope at first. But you trusted God and did your best, and God did great things through you. Help me believe that God has a plan for me, too. Amen.

September 4
Blessed Dina Bélanger
(April 30, 1897–September 4, 1929)

Feast Day: September 4

Patron of musicians

Dina was born in Quebec City, Canada. Her parents were devout Catholics who taught her how to pray, and Dina began to live the Gospel from a young age. The family did charitable work for other, less fortunate families. Dina's parents also made sure their daughter knew how to behave well. One day, when Dina was throwing a tantrum, her father joined her. She saw for the first time how silly it looked to throw a tantrum. So she stopped!

From an early age, Dina showed great musical talent. She began formal piano lessons at the age of eight. When she was nineteen years old, she enrolled at the Institute of Musical Art in New York City. She studied there for two years and stayed at the convent of the Religious of Jesus and Mary. Living there helped her to develop her prayer life. When she returned home to Quebec, she gave many concerts to help various charitable causes. She also taught music and was well loved by her students.

But Dina had heard the call of Christ to follow him in the religious life. When she was twenty-four, she entered the Religious of Jesus and Mary in Sillery, Quebec. She took the name Marie Sainte-Cecile of Rome. She continued to teach music, but her health was poor. She fell ill with tuberculosis and died when she was only thirty-two.

It seemed that Dina's short life would pass unnoticed by the world. But her superiors had asked her to write a spiritual autobiography. She obeyed, and through this book she touched many people. Her teaching was profound. It centered on how she lived in union with Jesus and the whole Trinity. But most of all, Dina showed how each person is called to be holy and united with Jesus in love.

Blessed Dina, you used music to help others learn about the beauty of God. Pray for me, that I may use my talents to glorify God just as you did. Amen.

September 5

Saint Teresa of Kolkata
(August 26, 1910–September 5, 1997)

Feast Day: September 5

Patron of the Missionaries of Charity and the poor

Agnes Gonxha Bojaxhiu was born in present-day North Macedonia. When she was eighteen years old, she entered the Loreto Sisters in Ireland. In 1929 she was sent to India. She made her first vows two years later and was called Sister Mary Teresa. She was asked to teach in the order's high school for girls. The students at the school were from wealthy families. But Teresa's heart was pained at the sight of the great poverty she observed in the city. There were many poor people living and dying on the streets with no one to take care of them.

In 1946 Teresa was traveling by train to make her yearly retreat. She had a mystical experience on the train and heard Jesus speaking to her heart. He told her of his compassion and love for the poor. Jesus asked Teresa to come and be his light in the service of the poor. For the next two years, she kept praying about how to respond to this call of Jesus. She asked her spiritual director and received permission to leave the Loreto Sisters to follow this new call. It was hard for her to leave the Loreto Sisters, but she did so in 1948.

Teresa went out into the streets and found the sick and the dying. She brought them to a house and cared for them, showing them the love Jesus felt for them. Before long, other young women joined her. It was the beginning of a new order called the Missionaries of Charity. Their mission was to bring Jesus to the poor and the most abandoned.

Mother Teresa, as she was called, went all over the world. Her work spread rapidly and she became famous, even receiving the Nobel Peace Prize. But through all this she remained simple and humble, always at the service of the poor. In her prayer she heard Jesus repeating the words he said on the cross, "I am thirsty." She tried to quench that thirst of Jesus for the rest of her life by bringing the Gospel to people through her service to the poor.

Saint Teresa, you dedicated yourself completely to serving Jesus in the poor. Pray for us so that we too might give of ourselves and of our goods to help those in material or spiritual need. Amen.

September 6
Blessed Bertrand of Garrigues
(c. 1195–1230)

Feast Day: September 6

Bertrand was born in France during a time when his country was troubled by religious wars. There was great confusion about Church teaching. Many people believed in false teachings called heresies. Bertrand's parents managed to live a peaceful life, and they taught the true faith to their son. But Bertrand saw the harm that the heresies were doing. When he was a boy, Cistercian monasteries were being attacked and persecuted because the monks were teaching people about the true Catholic faith. This left a deep impression on Bertrand. He decided early on that he wanted to be a priest, too.

Bertrand became a Cistercian and a priest. He spent his time helping people know the faith and come back to the Church. Then he met Saint Dominic and the two became good friends. This was God's invitation to Bertrand to begin a very important ministry. He was one of the six men who joined Dominic in 1215 to form a new religious congregation, the Order of Preachers, or Dominicans. Their goal was to teach people the truth about God and the Catholic Church. Bertrand was sent to Paris to start a house for the Order there. He also went with Dominic on many trips around Europe. He and Dominic got along very well with each other. People would say that Bertrand was a lot like Dominic—they were both very holy and loved God with their whole hearts. And they both wanted to share Christ's truth with everyone.

Meanwhile, the Order of Preachers was growing quickly. Dominicans were preaching the Gospel message in the towns and in the countryside. They had a big meeting, called a general chapter, in 1221. Bertrand was there. The Order was divided into eight provinces so that things could be run more effectively. Bertrand was put in charge of southern France. He spent the rest of his life preaching and helping the people there grow closer to God. He died of an illness in 1230. Soon after, many miracles began to happen through his intercession.

Blessed Bertrand, you and Saint Dominic were good friends and you became holy together. Help me remember to pray for my friends, too, especially when they are having a hard time. Amen.

September 7
Blessed John Duckett
and Blessed Ralph Corby
(John Duckett: 1603–September 7, 1644;
Ralph Corby: March 25, 1598–September 7, 1644)
Feast Day: September 7

Both John Duckett and Ralph Corby were priests. They lived in England at a time when Catholicism was illegal and no priests were allowed to be in the country.

John was raised as a Protestant, but then he converted to Catholicism. He went to college and became a priest in

1639. He studied for three more years in Paris and spent several hours each day in prayer. He knew it was dangerous in England, so before he went back, he spent two months with the Cistercian monks, devoting that time to prayer and retreat. The young priest labored for a year in England. But then he was caught with holy oils and a book of rites. When his captors threatened to hurt his family and friends if he did not tell them who he was, he admitted that he was a priest. He was brought to prison in London.

In prison, he met a fellow priest, Ralph Corby. Ralph was a Jesuit. He had been working in England for twelve years before he was caught celebrating Mass. The Jesuit Order tried very hard to get Ralph out of prison. When they were finally able to have him pardoned, he insisted that John should be the one to be reprieved, since John was younger. But John refused to walk away and leave his friend alone.

Actually, neither priest would have been allowed to escape. The judges ignored the reprieve and condemned both men to death. On September 7, 1644, at ten o'clock, the two friends mounted the cart that would take them to Tyburn, the scene of their execution. The people who saw them were struck by their holiness and cheerfulness. John and Ralph were at peace because they knew they were dying for Christ and would be with him soon. Before they died, they both made a short speech, then embraced each other. They would meet again in heaven.

Blesseds John Duckett and Ralph Corby, you gave a great witness by being joyful in the face of death. This was because your happiness was rooted in Christ. May we spread joy by the way we live our lives so that everyone will know Jesus through us. Amen.

Blessed Josefa Ruano García and Blessed Dolores Puig Bonany

(Josefa Ruano García: July 9, 1854–September 8, 1936;
Dolores Puig Bonany: July 11 or 12, 1857–September 8, 1936)

Feast Day: September 8

These sisters were martyrs of the Spanish Civil War. They spent their lives serving the poor and the elderly. Their generosity helped many people experience God's love.

Josefa and Dolores were born in Spain in the 1850s. Josefa grew up in a working-class family in Almería. Dolores was raised in Barcelona. Josefa entered the Congregation of the Little Sisters of the Abandoned Elderly in 1877 at age twenty-three. Dolores entered nine years later at age twenty-nine. They were among the first women to join this new community. The Little Sisters were founded in 1873 by Mother Teresa Jornet, who is now a saint. Their mission was to care for the poor and lonely elderly people in Spain.

Josefa and Dolores were patient, generous women. They helped the elderly feel safe and loved by God. Josefa also had a gift for leadership. She served as superior in three of the Congregation's houses. In 1934, she became superior in Requena. In 1936, Dolores also moved to the Requena community.

That same year, Spain broke out in civil war. Two major groups fought to control the country. One of them blamed the Church for the problems in Spain. They encouraged violence against Catholics. The Little Sisters knew they were in danger but chose to keep serving the poor and the elderly anyway. They would not leave the people who needed them.

The sisters encouraged each other and asked Jesus for strength.

On July 26, 1936, some soldiers went to the sisters' home in Requena. They ordered the sisters to leave and destroyed their chapel. After the soldiers left, some kind people welcomed the sisters into their homes. But one month later, the soldiers returned. They arrested Josefa, Dolores, and another sister named Gregoria. On September 8, 1936, they shot all three sisters. Josefa and Dolores died instantly. Gregoria survived to tell the world what happened. Josefa and Dolores were immediately praised as martyrs.

Blesseds Josefa and Dolores, you loved everyone with the heart of Jesus. You even gave your lives for them, like Jesus did. Help me love others as Jesus loves them. Amen.

September 9

Saint Peter Claver
(1581–September 8, 1654)

Feast Day: September 9

Patron of Colombia, African Americans, and racial justice

Peter was born in Spain and decided early on that he wanted to be a Jesuit priest. While he was still studying to become a Jesuit, he felt a burning desire to go to South America as a missionary. He volunteered and was sent to the seaport of Cartagena in Colombia. There, great shiploads of African slaves were brought to be sold.

At the sight of the people all crowded together, sick and suffering, Peter felt great pity. He made up his mind to help them and tell them about Jesus. As soon as a shipload arrived, he would go among the hundreds of sick slaves. He gave them food and medicine. He baptized the dying and the little babies. He nursed the ill. It was hard work in terrible heat. One man who went with Peter once could never face the heartbreaking sight again. Yet Peter did it for almost forty years. He baptized some three hundred thousand people. He cared for and loved those who were treated so unjustly by society.

Although the slave owners tried to stop Peter, he taught the faith to the slaves anyway. It was slow, discouraging work. Many people criticized him, saying it was all a waste of time. They thought the slaves would never keep the faith. But Peter was patient and he trusted that God would bless his people. He also went to visit his converts after they left Cartagena. The priest never stopped urging the slave owners to take care of the souls of their slaves and to be better Christians themselves.

During the last four years of his life, Peter was so sick that he had to stay in his room. He could not even celebrate Mass. Almost everyone forgot about him, but he never complained. Then suddenly when he died, it was like the whole city woke up. They realized that they had lost a saint. From then on, many people prayed through his intercession. Peter became known as the "apostle of the slaves."

Saint Peter Claver, you knew that God loves everyone, regardless of their race, religion, or culture. Help us love everybody as God's children and treat all people with equal respect. Amen.

September 10
Saint Nicholas of Tolentino
(c. 1245–September 10, 1305)

Feast Day: September 10

Patron of the souls in purgatory, and against fire and epidemic disease

Nicholas was born in central Italy. His parents had waited long and anxiously for a child. Nicholas was the answer to their prayers. As Nicholas grew up, he wanted to live close to God and be a priest. Friends of his family wanted him to be a priest in a wealthy parish where he would be promoted. Nicholas did not argue, but he quietly searched and prayed about what God wanted him to do.

One day, he heard a sermon from an Augustinian priest. He was very inspired by the sermon and realized how God had used that preacher to touch his own life. He became convinced of the importance of preaching God's word, and he decided to join the Augustinian Order, the same order that priest belonged to. Nicholas professed his vows when he was eighteen and became a priest a few years later. He performed his preaching ministry with love in various parishes. Then while praying in church one day, he seemed to hear a voice telling him to go to Tolentino. Shortly afterward, he was assigned to the town of Tolentino. He spent the remaining thirty years of his life there.

There was great political unrest in those times. Many people did not come to church or pay attention to God. The friars decided that they needed to go out and preach in the streets. Nicholas was chosen to be part of this initiative. He preached outside and in gathering places willingly. People listened, and many repented of their sins and led better lives. Nicholas spent hours in the poor areas of Tolentino. He visited the lonely. He brought the sacraments to the sick and dying. He took care of the needs of children and visited prisoners. Many miracles were reported, even while he was still alive. Once, he touched a sick child and asked God to heal him. The child was cured on the spot.

Nicholas was about sixty years old when he died of an illness.

Saint Nicholas of Tolentino, you listened to God's call in your heart, and many people found God because of this. Help me be a good listener to God's voice like you were. Amen.

September 11
Saint John Gabriel Perboyre
(January 6, 1802–September 11, 1840)
Feast Day: September 11

John was one of eight children born into a farming family in France. They were strongly rooted in the Catholic faith. One of John's uncles, who was a priest, had started a high school for boys who wanted to become priests. John's younger brother Louis entered this school. Their parents asked John to go and stay with Louis while he got used to living in a new place. To his surprise, John found that he liked the school and wanted to stay.

The idea of becoming a priest had taken root in John. As he grew older, his relationship with God got stronger and he became even more sure of his vocation. Eventually both John and his brother Louis were ordained priests. They belonged to the Congregation of the Mission, also known as the Vincentians.

John wanted to go to China, but at first he was given other duties in France. Meanwhile, Louis was sent to China for mission work. Sadly, he died on his journey there. So John asked his superiors if he could take his brother's place. They agreed.

In August 1835 John arrived in Macau. He started to study Chinese. Soon after, he was sent to Ho-Nan and then Hubei in central China. John tried to adapt himself to the Chinese culture so that he could better reach the people there. He shaved his head and wore a long pigtail as was the Chinese custom. He served the people and taught them about God's love and the Catholic faith. But the Chinese government was suspicious of Christians at that time. A persecution broke out and John was caught.

After his arrest, John was badly treated and put in prison. He was there for about a year. John suffered greatly, but he offered his pain up to God in prayer. He knew that Jesus understood his pain because Jesus had suffered on the cross to save us. This gave John great comfort. Finally, John was killed for his faith. In his martyrdom, he gave the ultimate witness to Jesus Christ.

Saint John, even though it was hard, you adapted yourself to foreign customs in order to share the Gospel. Help us to learn how to show others respect even if they are different from us. May the light of the Gospel shine through our words and deeds. Amen.

September 12

Blessed Frédéric Ozanam

(April 23, 1813–September 8, 1853)

Feast Day: September 9

Patron of social workers

Frédéric was born into a devout French Catholic family. As a teenager he struggled with doubts about the faith. But a priest he knew, Father Noirot, helped him through this crisis. Frédéric went to Paris to study law. He was not afraid to talk to the other students about matters of faith. When he was twenty years old, Frédéric put his faith into action by organizing a group to visit and help poor families. This became the Saint Vincent de Paul Society, which is now active throughout the world. A Daughter of Charity, Blessed Rosalie Rendu, helped in this work and gave him advice.

After obtaining his law degree, Frédéric taught at the university in Lyon. On June 23, 1841, he married Amelie Soulacroix. The couple had one daughter. They returned to Paris, where Frédéric continued teaching. He was a great scholar who was at home in the university as well as in the houses of the poor. His great concern, however, was his passion for social justice. And that grew out of his great love for Jesus Christ and for each person. Frédéric saw the face of Christ in the poor and the sick. He took to heart the words of Jesus, "just as you did it to one of the least of these who are members of my family, you did it to me" (Mt 25:40). Frédéric knew that the way we treat others is the way we treat Jesus.

Frédéric lived an intense life, always anxious to do as much as he could for the sake of the Gospel. But his health had never been very good and he died when he was forty years old.

Blessed Frédéric, your heart was moved with compassion at the plight of the poor. Pray for us so that we can have hearts that are attentive to the needs of others. Help us to reach out to people who are suffering from sadness or loneliness. Amen.

September 13
Saint John Chrysostom
(c. 347–September 14, 407)

Feast Day: September 13

Patron of education, public speakers, and those with epilepsy

John was born in Antioch, a part of the Roman Empire. His father died when he was a baby. John's mother chose not to marry again. She gave all her attention to bringing up her son and daughter. She made many sacrifices so that

John could have the best teachers. He was very intelligent and could have become a great man in the world. When he gave speeches, everyone loved to listen to him. In fact, his name, Chrysostom, means "golden-mouthed." Yet John wanted to give himself to God.

John decided to live a life of quiet prayer and discipline as a monk. But his health was not good; he could not live such a strict lifestyle. He chose instead to serve God as a priest. After several years of preaching and ministry, John was asked to be the bishop of the great city of Constantinople.

John was a wonderful bishop. Although he was always sick, he accomplished a tremendous amount of good. He preached once or twice every day. Many of his homilies were written down and are still read today. John also fed the poor and took care of orphans. He loved everyone, but he would not stand for sin. He was not even afraid to tell the empress when she was wrong.

Because John spoke out against sin and injustice, some people did not like him. The empress was one of them. She had John sent away from Constantinople. At first, John could write letters and stay in contact with the Church in Constantinople. Then he was exiled even further away. John was not strong enough to make the trip. Weakened from his travels, he died in present-day Turkey. But even then, John was happy to suffer for Jesus. He had given glory to God with his life. He wanted to do the same with his death.

Years later, John's body was brought back to Constantinople. The empress' son honored John's body and showed how sorry he was for what his mother had done. The people of Constantinople were happy to be reunited with their beloved saint.

Saint John Chrysostom, people loved to listen to your speeches.
You understood the power of words and the good they can do.
Help me to use my words to tell the truth and spread kindness.
May I show my love for God by the way I speak. Amen.

September 14
Saint Helena
(c. 246/48–c. 328)

Feast Day: August 18

Patron of archeologists

We do not know much about Helena's early life. At some point she met Constantius, a Roman soldier who later became the emperor. They got married and had one son, whom they named Constantine. However, Constantius divorced Helena and sent her and their son away. But after his father died, Constantine became the new emperor.

Constantine loved his mother very much and made sure she had an important place at the court. Then Helena converted to Christianity. The Romans had often persecuted the Christians. But in 313 Constantine won an important battle. He reportedly saw a cross in the sky beforehand and the words, "In this sign you shall conquer." After that, Constantine legalized Christianity in the Roman Empire.

Once she was a Christian, Helena wanted to go on a pilgrimage to the Holy Land to search for the actual cross that Jesus had died on in Jerusalem. Previously, the Romans had conquered Jerusalem and destroyed it. They had built a Roman temple on Mount Calvary, the place where Jesus died. Helena had this temple torn down. Workers began digging to find the cross. They found not one but three crosses, along with the sign that said that Jesus was king of the Jews. According to tradition, in order to find out which one was Jesus' cross, Helena brought in a sick woman who was near the point of death. The woman touched the first two crosses and nothing happened. But when she touched the third cross, she was suddenly healed. Helena knew that only the cross of Jesus would have such healing power.

Helena went on to discover other relics, said to be the nails from the cross and the holy tunic Jesus wore. Later on, Constantine had the Church of the Holy Sepulchre built on Calvary so that people could go to pray where Jesus had died. Helena brought large parts of Jesus' cross back to Rome with other relics. She also had other churches built at holy sites. She remained faithful to God her whole life.

Saint Helena, your love for Jesus led you on a search for the true cross. When problems and trials come into our lives, help us offer them up to Jesus in union with his cross. Help us not to complain but to do everything in union with Jesus. Amen.

September 15
Saint Catherine of Genoa
(1447–September 15, 1510)

Feast Day: September 15

Patron of brides, widows, and difficult marriages

Catherine was born into a wealthy Italian family. She married Giuliano Adorno, but it turned out to be a difficult marriage. Her husband spent a lot of their money and was not faithful to Catherine. This went on for about ten years. Catherine tried to find happiness by wasting her time with frivolous things, but she still felt unhappy. Then, in March 1473, she went to the sacrament of confession. While she was confessing her sins, she felt God's incredible love. At the same time, she realized how bad her sins were. She was overjoyed by God's love but deeply sorry for her sins. She was so overcome with awe that she could not finish her confession.

For the next three days, Catherine prayed and asked God to lovingly reveal all her faults. Then she went back to confession. She gave herself totally to the God who loved her and resolved not to sin anymore. From that point on, she began to pray more often and grew more and more holy.

Catherine was a mystic who had intense prayer experiences. She received special revelations from God, especially about purgatory. Catherine's intense experience of God's love in confession helped her explain purgatory in a positive way. She understood purgatory as a state after death where a person is purified from all selfishness and learns to love God completely.

Catherine also became the director of a large hospital in Genoa. By this time, her husband had converted to a better way of life. He helped Catherine with her holy works. Together they cared for the poor and the sick. Catherine also wrote down many of her teachings on the spiritual life. These were collected by her followers and published after her death in 1510. They are still read today.

Saint Catherine, pray for us that we too may understand and experience God's tremendous love for us. Help us to love God and others with our whole heart and soul. Amen.

September 16
Saint Cornelius and Saint Cyprian
(Cornelius: Unknown–253; Cyprian: c. 200–September 14, 258)

Feast Day: September 16

Cornelius: Patron of cattle and against epilepsy and ear ailments; Cyprian: Patron of Algeria and North Africa

In the middle of the third century, the Church was still being persecuted. The fierce persecution of Emperor Decius claimed the life of the Pope, Saint Fabian. The Church was without a pope for nearly a year. A holy priest of Rome, Cornelius, was elected to be the new pope in 251. He knew it might cost him his life, but he accepted because he loved Jesus and wanted to serve the Church. Because of this, Cornelius was greatly admired throughout the world.

The bishops of Africa were especially outspoken in their love and loyalty to the Pope. Cyprian, the bishop of Carthage, was one of them. He sent Cornelius letters of encouragement and support. Cyprian had not been born into a Christian family. He received a good education and became a lawyer for many years. Then he heard about Jesus and the message of Christianity. He decided to be baptized. Once he was a Christian, Cyprian wanted to totally dedicate his life to God. He became a priest, and in 249 he was made a bishop.

As bishop, Cyprian sent many letters. Some of them still exist today. Cyprian's writings explain the love that Christians should have for the whole Church. This love should be for the Pope as well as for the local diocese and parish. He also wrote very passionately about Church unity. The Church is the Body of Christ. Jesus is one, so the Church should be one, too. This was what Jesus wanted and prayed for at his Last Supper. And this is what Cyprian tried to tell people whenever divisions in the Church arose.

Cornelius had only been the Pope for two years when he died in exile at the port of Rome. Because he suffered so much as Pope, he is considered a martyr. Cyprian died five years later during the persecution of Emperor Valerian. He was beheaded at Carthage, the city where he had been bishop. Cornelius and Cyprian share a feast day to remind us of the importance of unity in the Church.

Saints Cornelius and Cyprian, you both worked for unity in the Church. Please look after the Pope and the bishops all over the world. May my own parish and diocese be blessed by God. And may the Church united as one in Jesus. Amen.

September 17

Saint Robert Bellarmine

(October 4, 1542–September 17, 1621)

Feast Day: September 17

Patron of catechists and catechumens

Robert was born in Italy. His family was noble, but they did not have a lot of money. His mother made sure he and his nine brothers and sisters were raised in the faith.

As a teenager, Robert went to a school run by Jesuits. He was very smart and did well in his studies. His father wanted him to be a doctor. But Robert had his heart set on joining the Jesuits and becoming a priest. For a whole year, Robert worked to persuade his father. At last, when Robert was eighteen, he was permitted to join the Jesuits.

As a young Jesuit, Robert studied, but he also taught others. He was sent to preach even before he became a priest. Once he was ordained in 1570, he continued teaching and preaching. Robert was a good teacher. He worked hard to prepare his lesson plans and help his students. People also loved to hear his sermons. Soon, Robert's superiors noticed how talented he was. They assigned him to be an important theologian in Rome.

This was just one of the ways Robert served the Church during his life. He also traveled to many places on behalf of the Pope. He settled arguments about correct Church teaching. And he wrote numerous books about the Catholic faith, including a catechism. In 1599, the Pope made Robert a cardinal. A few years later, Robert was named the archbishop of Capua, Italy.

Even with all these important tasks, Robert remained humble. He prayed often and lived a simple lifestyle. He especially loved the poor. When he had no money to give them, he found other creative ways to meet their needs. The Pope had given Robert a nice place to live. When poor people in rags came to visit him there, they would leave wearing the fine tapestries that were supposed to be hanging on his walls! When someone complained about this, Robert's response was simple: the walls would not get cold. The poor would.

Robert was seventy-nine when he died in Rome. He was later declared a doctor of the Church.

Saint Robert Bellarmine, you were very smart, but you did not brag about yourself or put others down. Instead, you humbly loved those under your care. Remind me that loving and caring for people is more important than being the best or beating others. Amen.

Saint Joseph of Cupertino

(June 17, 1603–September 18, 1663)

Feast Day: September 18

Patron of astronauts, pilots, and taking tests

Joseph was born in a small Italian village to poor parents. He was very unhappy as a boy and a teenager. His mother considered him a nuisance and treated him harshly. Joseph soon became very slow and absentminded. He would wander around as if he were going nowhere. He had a temper, too, and so he was not very popular.

As a teenager, Joseph tried to learn the trade of shoemaking, but failed. He asked to become a Franciscan, but they would not accept him. Next, he joined the Capuchin Order. But he could not seem to do anything right. He dropped piles of dishes and kept forgetting to do what he was told. After a few months, they sent him home. Joseph's mother was not pleased to have her eighteen-year-old son living at home again. She finally got him accepted as a helper at the Franciscan monastery.

Joseph was given the Franciscan habit to wear and was assigned to take care of the horses. About this time, Joseph began to change. He grew humbler and gentler. He became more careful and successful at his work. He also prayed more and lived with more discipline. Because of his progress, Joseph was allowed to become a member of the Franciscan Order and start his studies for the priesthood. Studying was very hard for Joseph. But he trusted in God's help and was eventually ordained a priest in 1628.

As time went on, Joseph became very holy. Everything he saw made him think of God. God began to work miracles through Joseph while he prayed. More than seventy times, people saw Joseph rise from the ground while saying Mass or praying. He would float near the ceiling, but he would not even notice because he was completely wrapped up in talking with God.

Joseph became so famous for his miracles that he was kept hidden. But Joseph did not mind. He was happy for the chance to be alone with the God he loved so much. Joseph was sixty years old when he died of an illness.

Saint Joseph of Cupertino, it took you a while to find your place in the world. When I feel like I do not belong, help me remember how much God loves me. Make me confident that Jesus has a plan for my life, even if I cannot see it yet. Amen.

September 19
Saint Januarius
(c. 275–c. 305)

Feast Day: September 19

Patron of blood donors and volcanic eruptions

Januarius lived in Roman Empire during the fourth century. He was born either in Benevento or Naples, Italy. He was the bishop of Benevento when Emperor Diocletian's persecution of the Church began.

According to tradition, Januarius learned that some Christian deacons had been put in prison for their faith. Januarius was a gentle, compassionate man. He was a good bishop who truly cared about his people. So, even though it was dangerous, he went to the prison to visit the deacons. The jailer saw what Januarius was doing and reported him to the governor. Soon, soldiers were sent to find him. Januarius was arrested along with a deacon and a lector. They joined the other Christians in prison.

Januarius and his companions were martyred for their faith. Legend says that they were taken to the amphitheater to be killed in front of a crowd. At first, the soldiers released bears into the amphitheater so that the prisoners would be torn to pieces. But the bears refused to attack the holy men. The soldiers were forced to behead Januarius and his friends instead. Their deaths took place near Naples in 305.

Since then, the people of Naples have claimed a special love for and devotion to Januarius, known in Italian as "San Gennaro." People pray for miracles through his intercession. One of the most well-known miracles involves a vial of Januarius' blood. This blood was preserved centuries ago and had become dark and dry. But at certain times of the year, the blood miraculously liquefies. It becomes red, sometimes bright red. At times, it even bubbles. This special miracle reminds us that God does not forget those who die for love of him. Today, this vial of blood is kept at the cathedral in Naples.

Saint Januarius, you are already in heaven with God. You want us to join you one day. Share with us the courage and love that made you into a bold martyr. May we serve God with all our hearts and be with him forever in heaven. Amen.

September 20

Saint Andrew Kim Taegŏn
and Saint Paul Chŏng Hasang

(Andrew Kim Taegŏn: August 21, 1821–September 16, 1846;
Paul Chŏng Hasang c. 1795–September 22, 1839)

Feast Day: September 20

Patrons of Korea

Andrew Kim Taegŏn was a priest and Paul Chŏng Hasang was a layperson. These two martyrs represent 113 Catholics who died for their faith in Korea.

Christianity reached Korea in the seventeenth century. It was brought there by laypeople. The believers nourished their faith with the word of God. They quietly grew and flourished. Then missionary priests came from France. The Korean people were introduced to the sacramental life of the Church. They were persecuted by the government throughout the nineteenth century. A total of 103 Koreans were killed between 1839 and 1867. Ten members of the Foreign Mission Society of Paris were martyred, too: three bishops and seven priests. This brought the total to 113.

Andrew Kim Taegŏn was from a family of farmers who had converted to Catholicism. He was baptized when he was fifteen years old. Andrew wanted to become a priest, but he could not receive his training in Korea. He traveled to Macao, China, and went to seminary there. Then he was ordained and returned home. He was the first native-born Korean priest. About a year later, Andrew was arrested for trying to help Catholic missionaries enter the country. He was only twenty-five when he became a martyr for the faith.

Paul Chŏng Hasang was also raised in a Catholic family. His father wrote the first Korean catechism and was martyred when Paul was a little boy. As Paul grew up, his family was persecuted for their faith. But this only made them love Jesus even more. Paul went to China as a young man to learn more about the faith. While he was there, he encouraged Catholic missionaries to come to Korea. He helped the missionaries with their work. He also taught people about their faith as a lay catechist. He was thinking about becoming a priest, but then a harsher persecution broke out. Paul was arrested, but he would not deny Jesus. After much suffering, Paul was martyred.

Saint Andrew Kim Taegŏn and Saint Paul Chŏng Hasang, we might not die for our faith the way you did, but we are called like you to introduce others to Jesus. Help us be good witnesses to our faith so that people can get to know Jesus through us. Amen.

September 21
Saint Matthew
(Unknown–First Century)

Feast Day: September 21

Patron of accountants and bankers

Matthew was a tax collector in the city of Capernaum, where Jesus was living. He was Jewish but he was working for the Romans, who had conquered the Jews. For this reason, his countrymen disliked him. They would not have anything to do with these "public sinners," as tax collectors were often called.

But Jesus did not feel that way about Matthew. One day, Jesus saw Matthew sitting in his office and he said, "Follow me" (Mt 9:9). At once, Matthew left his money and his position to follow Jesus. Then Matthew gave a big supper for Jesus. He invited other friends like himself to meet Jesus and listen to him teach.

Some people were upset about this. They did not think Jesus should be eating with people like Matthew who were considered sinners. They complained to Jesus' disciples. But Jesus overheard them and replied that only sick people need to go to a doctor. He meant that sinners were the ones who needed God's healing and forgiveness the most. So of course Jesus would spend time with Matthew and his friends! To this, he added, "I have come to call not the righteous but sinners" (Mt 9:13). In other words, only people who know they need God can be followers of Jesus. He cannot heal us if we refuse to admit we need help. Matthew understood this. The people who criticized Jesus did not.

Matthew spent the rest of his life as a faithful follower of Jesus. He is said to be the one who wrote the Gospel of Matthew, which is the story of Jesus and his teachings. According to tradition, Matthew became a martyr for the faith after preaching the Good News about Jesus to many people.

Saint Matthew, Jesus looked past people's bad opinions about you and saw the person you could become. Help us avoid judging others. Teach us how to treat everyone with love and respect. May we avoid copying the wrong things people do without looking down on them. Amen.

September 22
Blessed Carlos Navarro Miquel
(February 11, 1911–September 22, 1936)

Feast Day: September 22

Carlos was born in Spain to a devout Catholic family. He was the youngest of four boys, and he also had a sister who became a Salesian sister. Even when he was young, Carlos thought about being a priest when he grew up. He entered the minor seminary (which was like a high school) in order to start preparing for the priesthood. Through prayer, Carlos realized that he was not just called to be a priest. God was also calling him to belong to a religious order.

Soon Carlos was accepted into the Piarist Fathers. Their mission was teaching in schools. Carlos was happy in the seminary and looked forward to the day when he could be a priest and give the sacraments to the people. That day finally arrived when he was ordained on August 4, 1935. After that, Carlos was sent to a town called Albacete to teach at the Piarist school there.

But trouble loomed on the horizon. At that time, Spain was going through a civil war. Some groups were very hostile to the Catholic Church. Carlos had to go into hiding because these anti-Catholic groups were hunting down priests. First, he stayed with a friendly family in Albacete. But he did not want to put them in danger. He went back to his own home and stayed with his parents instead.

One day, some men came to the house and demanded to know where Carlos was. His father tried to protect him. But when Carlos saw what was going on, he came to the men and told them he was a Piarist priest. They arrested him and held him prisoner. Meanwhile other priests had also been arrested. In the jail, they prayed together and encouraged one another. Then, at around two o'clock in the morning on September 22, they were driven to a remote area outside the town. They were lined up and shot to death.

Even in the face of death, Carlos continued trusting God. Over and over again, he declared his faith in Jesus as our God and King. Carlos was twenty-five when he became a martyr for Jesus.

Blessed Carlos, pray for us that we may never be afraid to say that we are Christians and that we love Jesus. May we show by our lives that we love Jesus and live according to his Gospel. Amen.

September 23

Saint Pio of Pietrelcina

(May 25, 1887–September 23, 1968)

Feast Day: September 23

Patron of teenagers, relief of stress, and against depression

Francesco Forgione was born into a poor family in Italy. He wanted to be a priest, so his father went to work in the United States in order to pay for his school. Francesco studied hard. His health, however, was not good. He suffered much from stomach problems. Yet he still felt that God was calling him to be a priest. Francesco persevered and entered the Capuchin Order, a branch of the Franciscans. He was ordained a priest in 1910. He became known as Padre Pio, or Father Pio.

God gave Padre Pio some special experiences. One of these was the stigmata, which he received in 1918. This meant that his body was marked with wounds like those Jesus suffered on the cross. Padre Pio was very humble about this and did not want people to think he was anyone special. He suffered a lot. Some people thought he was a fraud. For a while, his superiors forbade him from celebrating Mass in public and from hearing confessions. This was a great blow to him, yet he accepted it with humility and obedience. But in 1934 the truth won out and Padre Pio was again given permission to offer Mass and hear confessions.

Padre Pio spent many hours in the confessional. People flocked to him from all over the world. He had the gift of reading people's souls and knew how to give just the right advice that each person needed to help them make a good confession. Besides this, Padre Pio also organized building a hospital for the poor. He wanted to help people in all their needs, both in body and soul. The hospital was opened in 1956. Padre Pio entrusted the work of running the hospital to others so he could continue hearing confessions all day.

On September 23, 1968, Padre Pio died a peaceful death. He was canonized by Saint John Paul II in 2002.

Saint Pio, you spent a great deal of time helping people in confession to break away from sin. Pray for me that I might lead a holy life and never offend Jesus by any serious sin. Amen.

September 24
Blessed Émilie Tavernier-Gamelin
(February 19, 1800–September 23, 1851)

Feast Day: September 23

Émilie was born into a large family in Montreal, Canada. When she was only four, her mother died, so Émilie was raised by an aunt. Émilie always had a heart of compassion for the poor. As a teenager, she began taking care of one of her brothers whose wife had died. She would often invite poor people into their home for meals.

When she was twenty-three, Émilie married Jean-Baptiste Gamelin, who was fifty years old. Despite their age difference, the marriage was a good one. But it only lasted four years. Her husband died in 1827. They had had three children, but all of them died too. Émilie was very sad at the loss of her family. But she put even more energy into charitable works. She opened a home for abandoned women and then two more homes. Émilie used up all her money, but she trusted completely in God to provide for her. And God never let her down.

In 1833 a cholera epidemic struck Montreal. Émilie visited the sick in their homes. Then she started to take in orphans and to care for the mentally ill. She also visited prisoners and was called "The Angel of the Prisons."

The bishop of Montreal, Ignace Bourget, was happy to see all that Émilie was doing. Some women had already volunteered to help Émilie. The bishop wanted to start a religious community so that all these works could continue. The community was formed in 1843. The first group of sisters took religious vows a year later, and Émilie became the superior of the new community. They were eventually called the Sisters of Providence. Under Émilie's guidance, the group grew even more.

In 1851 another cholera epidemic struck the city. Émilie caught the disease and died. Her last words were, "Humility, simplicity, charity." She wanted her sisters to remember that charity, or love, was the most important thing. The religious community she left behind continued to grow. The Sisters of Providence can now be found all over the world.

Blessed Émilie, many difficult and sad things happened to you during your life. But you always saw that God was with you in your suffering. Help me remember that when things are difficult in my life, God is with me too. Amen.

September 25
Saint Cosmas and Saint Damian
(Unknown–c. 303)

Feast Day: September 25 (Canada); September 26

Patrons of doctors, nurses, and physicians

Cosmas and Damian were brothers, possibly twins, who were born in Syria during the third century. Not many details are known about their lives except from the stories that have been handed down about them. According to tradition, Cosmas and Damian were Christians who wanted to do something to help others and spread Jesus' love in the world. They both decided to study medicine in Syria. Then they moved to a part of the Roman Empire called Cilicia (modern-day Turkey). There, they became excellent doctors.

Cosmas and Damian saw every patient as a brother or sister in Christ. Because of this, they showed great love to all and treated people's sicknesses to the best of their abilities. But there was something unusual about these two doctors. They would not accept any money for their services, no matter how much care a patient required! This earned them a Greek nickname that means "the penniless ones." For Cosmas and Damian, helping others was more important than becoming rich.

Every chance they had, the two brothers told their patients about Jesus. The people loved and trusted Cosmas and Damian, so they listened to them willingly. This was Cosmas and Damian's way of taking care not only of people's bodies, but of their souls as well.

In 303, the Roman emperor Diocletian began persecuting Christians. Soon, the persecution reached the city where Cosmas and Damian were living. The brothers had never tried to hide their great love for their Christian faith, so they were arrested at once. They were tortured, but nothing could make them give up their belief in Jesus. They had lived for him and had brought so many people to his love. They were also willing to die for Jesus. Cosmas and Damian became martyrs together.

Saints Cosmas and Damian, you never charged money for taking care of people. Help me to do good deeds with a generous heart. Even when I am not rewarded for it, may I still do my best to help others. Amen.

September 26

Saint Jean de Brébeuf, Saint Isaac Jogues, and Companions

Saint Jean de Brébeuf (March 25, 1593–March 16, 1649),
Saint Isaac Jogues (January 10, 1607–October 18, 1646)

Feast Day: September 26 (Canada); October 19

Patrons of North America

The North American Martyrs were six French Jesuit priests and two laymen. They traveled mainly in Canada, bringing the Gospel to the native peoples there. They lived with the people, teaching them about Jesus. After much hard work, they helped many in the Huron tribe convert to Christianity. Some members of other tribes also converted. But enemies of the Hurons, such as the Iroquois and Mohawks, saw the Christian missionaries as their enemies, too. Between 1642 and 1649, they killed Jean and his companions.

Each of these martyrs showed heroic love and bravery. Jean de Brébeuf had tuberculosis. He was so sick in France that he could not even teach many classes. Yet this priest's courage amazed the Iroquois as they tortured him to death. Another priest named Gabriel Lalemant also died with him.

Isaac Jogues was a priest kidnapped by an enemy tribe. Later, he was freed and went back to France. But even though he had already suffered tortures, Isaac longed to continue working as a North American missionary. Soon after his return, he was killed by Mohawks. Two of Isaac's helpers were René Goupil and Jean de Lalande. They were faithful laypeople who also suffered martyrdom.

Antoine Daniel had just finished celebrating Mass in his Huron village when the Iroquois attacked. The Christian Hurons begged him to escape, but Antoine stayed and died with them. He would not abandon his people who were asking to be baptized before they were killed.

The missionary priest Charles Garnier was shot during a surprise attack. Despite his injury, he crawled to help a dying man. He was killed while absolving the man's sins. One of Charles' companions was a priest named Noël Chabanel. Noël found it difficult to live the hardships of missionary life. But he truly felt that was where God wanted him to be. He made a vow to stay in North America and kept it until the end, when he was also martyred.

The sacrifices of these brave missionaries were not in vain. After their deaths, the Gospel was brought to almost every tribe the martyrs had known.

Saint Jean and Saint Isaac, you and your companions gave your lives to help the people of North America become Christian. Please continue watching over us today. Help the people of North America to love God and live good lives in the service of others. Amen.

Saint Vincent de Paul

(April 24, 1581–September 27, 1660)

Feast Day: September 27

Patron of charities, horses, and the Saint Vincent de Paul Society

Vincent was the son of poor French farmers. One of his jobs as he was growing up was taking care of the family's pigs. But Vincent's father could see he was intelligent, so he sent his son to school. Vincent wanted to dedicate his life in service of God and the Church. So, after he had finished his studies, Vincent became a priest.

At first, Vincent was given an important position as the teacher of rich children, and he lived rather comfortably. Then one day, he was called to the side of a poor man who was dying. Once he heard the man's confession, Vincent realized how much the poor people of France needed better spiritual help. When he began to preach to them, whole crowds went to the sacrament of confession. He finally decided to start a congregation of priests to work especially among the poor. It was called the Congregation of the Mission.

Vincent involved himself in many other good works as well. He started so many different charities that it seems impossible for one person to have done so much! He took care of criminals who worked on the sailing ships. He started the Sisters of Charity with Saint Louise de Marillac. He opened hospitals and homes for orphans and old people. He collected large sums of money for poor areas, sent missionaries to many countries, and bought back prisoners of war.

Even though Vincent was a very charitable man, he humbly admitted that he would not have been able to do anything without God. He once said that God's grace was what improved his personality and made him such a loving, generous person. Vincent was seventy-nine when he died in Paris.

Saint Vincent de Paul, whenever you saw someone in need, you did everything you could to assist that person. I have many opportunities to help others and brighten their day. Teach me how to pay attention for these moments. Make me bold in being kind to others. Amen.

September 28

Saint Lorenzo Ruiz

(c. 1605–September 29, 1637)

Feast Day: September 28

Patron of the Philippines and the poor

Lorenzo was from Manila, in the Philippines. His mother was Filipina and his father was Chinese. When Lorenzo was growing up, he was taught by the Dominicans. He liked to help out at his local parish by altar serving or running errands for the priests. He had a special love for the Blessed Mother and prayed the Rosary often.

As a young man, Lorenzo married a woman named Rosario. He became the father of three children, two sons and a daughter. The family was a happy one, and they liked to pray together. But then disaster struck. It seems that Lorenzo was falsely accused of murdering someone. Many of the judges at that time were corrupt. Lorenzo knew that the court would not believe he was innocent. He had to run away to save his life.

While he was escaping, Lorenzo met a group of Dominicans. They were boarding a ship for a missionary journey. Lorenzo decided to go with them. He thought they were heading for China, but instead the group went to Japan. At that time, the persecution against Christians in Japan was very harsh. Still, Lorenzo decided to stay with the missionaries and help them minister to the Japanese Christians.

A few weeks after they arrived, Lorenzo and his companions were arrested for being Christian. They were told to give up their faith and suffered many tortures. Before Lorenzo died, he bravely declared that he was a Catholic. He said that if he had a thousand lives to give for God, he would.

Lorenzo and fifteen others were martyred in Nagasaki, Japan, between the years 1633 and 1637. The group was made up of nine Dominican priests, two Dominican brothers, and five laypeople. They were missionaries who had originally come from five nations—France, Italy, Japan, the

Philippines, and Spain. These heroic men and women were proclaimed saints on October 18, 1987.

Saint Lorenzo Ruiz, it might seem like you were in the wrong place at the wrong time. But God worked through your circumstances and you became a brave martyr for Jesus. Help us to trust in God's plan, no matter where it takes us. Amen.

September 29
Saint Michael, Saint Gabriel, and Saint Raphael

Feast Day: September 29

Michael: Patron of the military, paramedics, and police officers;
Gabriel: Patron of those who work in communications,
television, or radio; Raphael: Patron of nurses, travelers,
and the blind

Michael, Gabriel, and Raphael are called saints because they are holy. But they are different from the rest of the saints because they are not human. They are angels. They are protectors of human beings who love God totally. We know something about each of them from the Bible.

Michael's name means "Who is like God?" Three books of the Bible speak of Michael: Daniel, Revelation, and the Letter of Jude. In the book of Revelation, we read of a great war that went on in heaven (Rev 12:7–9). Michael was the leader of God's angels who battled with Satan. Michael became the champion of loyalty to God. He still guards the

Church today and is often invoked for protection against evil.

Gabriel's name means "God is my strength." He, too, is mentioned in the book of Daniel. He has become familiar to us because Gabriel is an important person in Luke's Gospel. God chose Gabriel to go to Nazareth and talk to Mary. Gabriel was the one who told Mary that she would be the mother of Jesus. Gabriel also visited Zechariah, the father of Saint John the Baptist. He announced the joyful news that Zechariah and his wife would have a son who would prepare the way for the Messiah. Gabriel is the announcer, the communicator of the Good News. He especially helps those who work in the field of communications.

Raphael's name means "God has healed." We hear about him in the Bible from the book of Tobit. Raphael brought protection and healing to the blind Tobit. He also helped Tobit's son find a good wife, traveling with him in disguise. At the very end of the journey, when all was completed, Raphael revealed his true identity. He called himself one of the seven angels who stand before God's throne. Raphael still protects those who are ill or going on a journey.

Michael, Gabriel, and Raphael are called archangels because they are especially important among the many angels in heaven. God has given us these heavenly helpers because he loves us.

Saint Michael, Saint Gabriel, and Saint Raphael, be with me today. Protect me from whatever could cause me spiritual or physical harm. Help me to be faithful to Jesus and a good communicator of his divine love. Amen.

September 30
Saint Jerome
(c. 347–September 20, c. 420)

Feast Day: September 30

Patron of archaeologists, archivists, and librarians

Jerome was a Roman Christian who lived in the fourth century. His father taught him about the faith but sent him to a famous Roman school. There, Jerome grew to love reading. But the books he liked were not written by Christians and they did not have any Christian values in them. They started to distract and confuse him. He made some bad decisions, seeking pleasure instead of trying to be a good person. But whenever he thought about God, Jerome felt like he was not living up to his full potential. Then he began spending time with a group of holy Christians. They became close friends and inspired Jerome to change his life around.

Jerome studied theology and languages so that he could put his intelligence at the service of Jesus. Later, he went to live in the desert where he could pray with fewer distractions. Jerome was still tempted by things from his old life sometimes. The immoral entertainment held in Rome seemed fresh in his imagination and memory. He missed the books he used to read. But Jerome did not give in. His simple, hard life of prayer helped him stay focused on God. He also studied more, filling his time with good activities. He wrote books and letters that defended and explained the faith. He helped to translate the Bible into Latin. Many more people were then able to read and enjoy it. Besides all this, Jerome offered spiritual advice to those who came to him.

Jerome spent long years of his life in a little cave at Bethlehem, where Jesus had been born. There he prayed, wrote, studied the Bible, and taught people how to serve God. But Jerome was by no means perfect. He was known for having a bad temper, and his sharp tongue made him many enemies. Still, he was a very holy man who spent his life trying to serve Jesus as best he could. And so, despite his temper, Jerome became a great saint.

Saint Jerome, you grew holy by finding good ways to spend your time. Teach us to pay attention to how we use our free time and what we do for fun. May we choose to do things that bring us closer to God and make us truly happy. Amen.

October 1
Saint Thérèse of Lisieux
(January 2, 1873–September 30, 1897)

Feast Day: October 1

Patron of France, florists, and missionaries

Thérèse was born in France and was the youngest daughter of Saints Louis and Zélie Martin. Thérèse was a very lively, lovable little girl. Her father called her his "little queen." Yet she could be too sensitive and irritable. She later said that the infant Jesus helped her overcome this weakness. Thérèse wanted to enter the Carmelite convent in Lisieux where two of her sisters were already nuns. But since she was only fifteen, she was not allowed. Thérèse felt sure that Jesus wanted her to spend her life loving him alone. She kept praying and asking the superior to admit her. She even dared to ask the Pope himself to grant her heart's desire. And finally, she was allowed to enter.

Although she was young, Thérèse did not expect to be babied. She wanted Jesus to make her a martyr in heart and body. And she meant it. During the winters, Thérèse suffered from the bitter cold and dampness of her plain bedroom. There were other kinds of sufferings, too. Whenever she was humiliated, she would offer her pain to her beloved Jesus and keep on smiling. Thérèse knew that no matter what happened, God loved her very much. She always had a burning desire to become a saint. She wanted to find a "shortcut," an "elevator" to heaven. She looked in the Bible and read about how much God loves those who are little and trust in him instead of themselves. Thérèse took this to heart and trusted God with everything. She called her great confidence in him her "little way" to holiness.

Soon, Thérèse became very sick. She knew she was dying, but she still had faith in God's love for her. She promised to send a shower of roses from heaven after she died. This is part of why she is called the Little Flower. She also said she would help people on Earth from heaven. Thérèse died when she was twenty-four years old. After her death, many miracles happened through her intercession.

Saint Thérèse, you offered every difficulty and sacrifice to Jesus, no matter how small. When I want to complain about something, help me instead to offer it up to Jesus with love. Amen.

October 2
Guardian Angels

Feast Day: October 2

Guardian angels are God's messengers who protect us human beings. Angels are not humans with wings (even though they are often shown this way in art). They are spiritual creatures who do not have bodies the way we do. Angels serve God in heaven and do special jobs for him. We see them throughout the Bible. For example, in the New Testament, the Acts of the Apostles tells about how Saint Peter was led out of prison by an angel sent by God (Acts 12:6–11). Jesus talked about angels too. Once he was speaking to his disciples about how precious children are to God. Jesus said, "Take care that you do not despise one of these little ones; for, I tell you, in heaven their angels continually see the face of my Father in heaven" (Mt 18:10).

Each of us has a guardian angel that sees God in heaven. This is a special gift from our loving God. Our angels stay with us during our whole lives. They help us listen to God. They also pray for us. They want us to come to heaven, too. Hopefully one day, we will be able to praise God together with the angels in heaven.

Since very early on, Christians have believed in guardian angels. But in 1608, Pope Paul V decided to make a special day for us to remember our guardian angels and thank God for them. It is very encouraging to know and believe that we each have an angel guarding and protecting us. We can ask our guardian angels for help whenever we are afraid or need extra prayers.

Guardian Angel, I know that you love me and want me to love God. Teach me how to love God a little more every day. Protect me from all dangers, so that someday we can be together with God in heaven. Amen.

October 3

Blessed Bartolo Longo
(February 10, 1841–October 5, 1926)

Feast Day: October 5

Bartolo was born in Latiano, a town in southern Italy. He grew up in a wealthy and well-educated Catholic family. But as a teenager, he started to drift away from the Church and his Catholic faith. By the time Bartolo was in college, he had completely rejected God. He started spending time with people who hated the Catholic Church. He even began praying to the devil rather than to Jesus.

Bartolo's family was frightened. They begged God to save him and bring him home to the Church. One of Bartolo's friends, a Catholic professor named Vincenzo Pepe, also saw how much danger Bartolo was in. Professor Pepe spoke to Bartolo many times. Finally, he helped Bartolo realize how lost he was. Bartolo spoke to a priest and went to confession. He was home at last.

But Bartolo still felt worried. He wondered if God had really forgiven him for all the evil he had done. He asked God what he should do. As he prayed, he remembered something a priest had told him about the power of the

Rosary. Bartolo knew this was his answer. God had truly forgiven him. Now, Bartolo would show his gratitude to God by teaching people to pray the Rosary. He knew that Mary would use this special prayer to lead many people to Jesus. He believed Mary would bring him closer to Jesus, too.

Bartolo wrote books and organized prayer groups. He spoke to people of all ages about Jesus and his Blessed Mother. He helped build the famous Basilica of Our Lady of the Most Holy Rosary of Pompeii. Bartolo's work touched many people. His writings even inspired Saint John Paul II to create the Luminous Mysteries of the Rosary.

Bartolo died in 1926. His last words were about how much he wanted to see Mary. He knew that Mary had helped him return to Jesus and his Church.

Blessed Bartolo Longo, you returned home to the Catholic Church because Mary prayed for you. Help me understand how much Mary loves and cares about me. Amen.

October 4
Saint Francis of Assisi
(c. 1181–October 3, 1226)

Feast Day: October 4

Patron of animals and animal rights, ecology, and peace

Francis was the son of a rich merchant in Assisi, Italy. Growing up, he loved parties and good times. But after becoming very ill and spending some time as a prisoner of war, Francis realized that he was wasting his life. He became aware that God loved him and felt that he should be serving Jesus instead of himself. He began to listen to God and pray regularly. Often, he gave his clothes and money to the poor. The he started fasting and dressing in rags to humble himself. It is not hard to imagine how his rich former friends must have reacted! His father was very angry with Francis' behavior and tried to get him to stop. Francis bore all this suffering for love of Jesus.

When his father took everything from him in disgust, Francis put all his trust in God, his Father in heaven. He began to live as a beggar. Everywhere he went, he urged people to stop sinning and return to God. Soon many men began to realize how holy Francis was, and they became his disciples. That is how the great Franciscan Order of priests and brothers began. Later, Francis also organized groups for women and laypeople. The Franciscans helped the poor and sick and preached everywhere. Even after the Order had spread all over Italy, Francis insisted that they should not own anything. He knew that poverty was a way of becoming closer to Jesus and trusting in God more.

One of the things Francis is known for is his love of nature and animals. He loved them because they were created by God for us to take care of. Sometimes the birds would even come listen to him preach!

A few years before Francis died, Jesus gave Francis his own wounds in his hands and feet. This is called the stigmata. It was a sign of Francis' union with the crucified Christ. Toward the end of his life, Francis became very sick. Before he died, he encouraged his brothers to love God, to love being poor, and to follow the Gospel.

Saint Francis of Assisi, you wanted to be happy more than anything in life. You found happiness when you made Jesus the center of your life. Help us to see what is really valuable in our lives and what is not. Amen.

October 5
Saint Maria Faustina Kowalska
(August 25, 1905–October 5, 1938)

Feast Day: October 5

Patron of mercy and those who are dying

Helena Kowalska was born into a hardworking and devout Polish family. She found a job as a maid to help support her family when she was sixteen. Even as a young girl, her faith was always important to her. She wanted to become a nun, but her parents did not give permission. When she was old enough, she entered the Congregation of the Sisters of Our Lady of Mercy. She took the name Maria Faustina.

Faustina lived a simple life in the convent. She did household chores such as cooking, cleaning, and gardening. But behind this simple exterior life, she lived a very deep mystical life. She had extraordinary experiences in which Jesus appeared to her and asked her to tell the whole world about God's mercy.

It was not an easy mission. At first, when Faustina explained her experiences to priests, they thought she was unwell. But Jesus sent her two good priests who believed her and guided her in this work. Part of her mission involved having an image painted of Jesus showing his mercy. It has two rays coming out from his heart. The red ray represents his precious Blood, and the white ray represents grace and the waters of Baptism. Jesus told Faustina that he would grant many graces to those who would show honor to the image. He also gave Faustina a special prayer called the Chaplet of Divine Mercy. He urged everyone to pray this Chaplet for the dying. He told her that the hour of his death, three o'clock, is the hour of great mercy. He promised he would grant immense graces to those who unite their prayers to his passion. Jesus also wanted to establish a feast of Divine Mercy on the Sunday after Easter.

Faustina died when she was only thirty-three years old. She had fulfilled her mission. It took time for the Church to approve her message. Saint John Paul II canonized Saint Faustina and extended the feast of the Divine Mercy to the whole Church.

Saint Faustina, you told people all about God's mercy. Help me to trust in the mercy of Jesus. Help me also to practice mercy by doing good deeds for others. Amen.

October 6

Blessed Marie-Rose Durocher

(October 6, 1811–October 6, 1849)

Feast Day: October 6

Patron of the sick and loss of parents

Eulalie Durocher was born in a little village near Montreal, Canada. She was the tenth of eleven children. Eulalie was active as a child, enjoying activities like horse-back riding. As she grew up, Eulalie thought about becoming a nun, but her health was not very good. Then when Eulalie was eighteen, her mother died. Eulalie's older brother, who was a priest, invited her to come stay at his parish in Beloeil. There, Eulalie found a way to serve God by helping her brother. She took charge of the household duties so that he could focus on being a good priest. She also became very active in the parish. During the thirteen years she was involved in the life of the Church and the parish, God was preparing her to do an important task.

In 1843, when Eulalie was thirty-two, the bishop of Montreal asked her to begin a very special mission. He wanted her to start a new community of sisters devoted to education. Eulalie was reluctant at first. She knew that more religious communities were needed to teach the children in rural areas. But she never thought she would be the one to do something about that! Besides this, her health was still not good. But despite her worries, Eulalie trusted that this was God's will for her. She founded the Sisters of the Holy Names of Jesus and Mary. Their particular work for Jesus was to educate the poorest and most neglected children. Eulalie became Mother Marie-Rose. Others followed this generous woman. They, too, believed in the importance of educating children for the love of Jesus.

Mother Marie-Rose lived only six years after her congregation began. However, she helped her sisters from heaven because the community continued to grow and open new convents. They started a mission in the United States, too. Today the Sisters of the Holy Names of Jesus and Mary are spread throughout the world.

Blessed Marie-Rose, you made many sacrifices to give children a good education. When my schoolwork is difficult or boring, help me to still try my very best. Amen.

October 7
Blessed Francis Xavier Seelos
(January 11, 1819–October 4, 1867)

Feast Day: October 5

Francis was born in Bavaria, Germany. His father was the sacristan at their parish church. Young Francis wanted to become a priest, so he went to school to study philosophy. In 1842 he entered the diocesan seminary. He learned about the great needs of the Church in the United States by reading letters from missionaries there. Many German-speaking immigrants had no priests. Francis' heart burned with a desire to help them. So he applied to the missionary Redemptorist Order and they accepted him. In 1843 he sailed to New York to continue his studies for the priesthood. He was ordained a priest in 1844 in Baltimore.

Francis was sent to Pittsburgh, Pennsylvania, where he worked for nine years. Saint John Neumann, another Redemptorist saint, was the superior of the community there. Francis got to know John well, and John gave him good guidance and spiritual direction. The Redemptorists gave many parish missions where they told everyone about God's love. Francis was an excellent preacher. He was also very kind to people in the confessional, giving them good advice. News about him spread and many people came to see him from all over. He heard confessions in English, German, and French, so he could minister to as many people as possible.

Starting in 1863, Francis spent three years as a traveling missionary priest. He worked in ten different states in the East and the Midwestern United States. His preaching style was simple. He talked about difficult topics in a way people could understand. In 1866 he was sent to New Orleans in Louisiana, but he would only spend about a year there. An epidemic of yellow fever spread throughout the city. Francis helped tend the sick. But then he caught the disease and died from it. He was beatified by Saint John Paul II in the year 2000.

Blessed Francis, your heart went out to people who needed a priest and you spent your life ministering to them. Pray for us so that we might see the needs of others around us and do what we can to help them. Amen.

October 8

Blessed Francisco de Paula Víctor

(April 12, 1827–September 23, 1905)

Feast Day: September 23

Patron of racial harmony

Francisco was born into slavery in Brazil. His mother's name was Lourença Justiniana de Jesus; his father is unknown. Francisco was baptized about a week after he was born. His godmother, Marianna Santa Barbara Ferreira, was the slave owner. Slavery is a great evil and no one can own another person. But Marianna at least treated the slaves with dignity and saw to it that Francisco was educated. He learned to read and write and was trained to be a tailor, or someone who makes or repairs clothes. But Francisco wanted to be a priest. No slave or Black man in Brazil had ever become a priest. But Francisco was determined. With God's help he did the impossible. Marianna let him go and he was admitted to the seminary.

Sadly, the other seminarians treated him badly because of his background and the color of his skin. But Francisco did not let this discourage him. He trusted in God and was ordained in 1851. He was sent to a parish and, while some of the people accepted him, many did not. They did not want to have a Black priest. But Francisco followed Jesus' command to love our neighbors, even those who do not like us. He was kind to everybody. Eventually he won over the people and they began to trust him because he was such a holy priest. When the bishop wanted to transfer him to another parish, the people who had at first rejected Francisco now protested that he should remain and be their priest.

Francisco is known as the "Apostle of Charity" because of the way he helped his flock, especially the poor. He set up a school named after the Holy Family. He welcomed everyone, no matter what color their skin was. He himself taught the children their catechism to give them a solid foundation in the faith. He also taught music and French. Francisco spent over fifty years in the same parish, giving his time and energy to God and the people he served until his death.

Blessed Francisco, you suffered much because of racial prejudice. Yet in your life, love overcame all difficulties. Help us to treat each person with love and respect no matter what they look like. Pray for us so that there may be no more racism in the world. Amen.

October 9

Saint John Henry Newman

(February 21, 1801–August 11, 1890)

Feast Day: October 9

Patron of Newman Centers on university campuses

John was born into an Anglican family in England and received an excellent education. From his youth he was devoted to prayer and study. He also wanted to serve people in a spiritual way. So he became an Anglican priest. Because of his brilliant mind, he studied at Oxford. It was an important center of learning. John was put in charge of the church there, named St. Mary the Virgin. He began to read and study the writings of early Christian authors. He also became involved with a group called the Oxford Movement. This group wanted to follow the teachings of the early Church more closely.

Gradually, this study led John to see that the Roman Catholic Church is the one Church that teaches what the early Church believed. This put John in a crisis, since he was a devout Anglican. He loved the Anglican Church and the thought of leaving it was hard for him. But he followed where the truth led him. John became a Roman Catholic in 1845. Then he went to Rome to study to become a Catholic priest. While there, he became a member of the Oratory of Saint Philip Neri, a spiritual group for priests that gave them spiritual support and provided a community.

John returned to England, but his life as a Catholic was difficult. Many of his former friends rejected him. Some of the Catholics did not trust him. They thought that he was still an Anglican at heart. John then wrote the story of his conversion, and it became a famous book. He wrote many other books too, as well as many letters. He helped to open the Catholic University of Ireland and held an important position there for seven years. He was a great intellectual. But as a priest, he was concerned with the needs of people. He wanted to minister to all.

In 1879, Pope Leo XIII made him a cardinal for his immense service to the Church. He died eleven years later, when he was eighty-nine years old.

Saint John Henry Newman, pray for us that we might always seek the light of the truth, which is found in Jesus Christ and his Church. Amen.

October 10
Saint Francis Borgia
(October 28, 1510–September 30, 1572)

Feast Day: September 30

Patron of protection from earthquakes

Francis was born into a prominent family in Spain. His family was well-connected socially and moved in the highest circles. He received a good education and had a bright future. He got married and he and his wife, Eleanor, had eight children. When his father died, Francis succeeded him as the fourth Duke of Gandía. He was a good Catholic, but his faith was not very strong.

In 1539 he had a conversion experience and became more fervent. It happened when the Empress Isabel died and Francis saw her corpse. She had been a beautiful woman, but her body was already decaying. The sight of it shocked Francis. He began to realize that earthly things do not last. In 1546, Eleanor died and Francis decided to enter the Jesuits. At that time Saint Ignatius, their founder, was still alive. Francis became good friends with Ignatius, who taught him how to live as a Jesuit.

In 1551 Francis was ordained a priest. He did a tremendous amount of work. He founded a dozen colleges in Spain so that people could receive a good Catholic education. He went to Rome and helped start a college there. It later became the Gregorian University, which still exists today. Later on, Francis was chosen to be the third Father General of the Jesuits. As superior over the whole religious order, his zeal grew even greater. He greatly expanded the Jesuits and many men entered the community. He sent Jesuits to begin new missions in America. He also continued to found new schools. But he is best known for his saintly life of virtue. He practiced the virtues of humility and charity and was greatly loved.

Francis was ill for a short time before his death and died at age sixty-one.

Saint Francis Borgia, you gave your life to God when you realized that earthly things are passing. Help me to keep the thought of heaven in mind, especially when I am facing some difficulty. Amen.

October 11
Saint John XXIII
(November 25, 1881–June 3, 1963)

Feast Day: October 11

Patron of papal delegates and the Second Vatican Council

Angelo Roncalli was born into a poor farming family in Bergamo, Italy. He became a priest when he was in his twenties. Soon after, he became an assistant to the bishop. Angelo also taught in the seminary, especially Church history. During World War I he was drafted into the Italian army. He served as a chaplain and helped the sick and wounded.

After the war, Angelo worked in Rome for the Vatican and also taught at the Lateran University. He was very humble and friendly and people liked him. Because of these talents, he was made a Vatican diplomat in 1925. He became a bishop and was sent to Bulgaria, a country in Southeast Europe. Later he served in Turkey and Greece, and became the apostolic nuncio—an official representative of the Pope—to France in 1944. As nuncio, Angelo used his influence to save many Jews from the Nazis during World War II.

Then, he was elected Pope in 1958 and took the name John. Because he was older (seventy-six), many people thought he would be Pope only for a short time. But he soon shocked everyone by calling an ecumenical council, the largest and most important type of meeting in the Catholic Church. In an ecumenical council, Church officials and theologians come from all over the world to discuss important questions and problems facing the Church today. John said that the Holy Spirit inspired him with the idea. One of the goals of this council, known as the Second Vatican Council or Vatican II, was to reach out to the modern world. But John did not live to see the whole council—he died about eight months after it began, at the age of eighty-one.

Throughout his life, John always sought to do God's will. He took the motto "obedience and peace." Even when he was the Pope, he did not expect any special treatment. Known for his smile and his sense of humor, John lived in simplicity and joy.

Saint John XXIII, pray for me that I too may see the image of God in each person whom I meet and treat them with kindness. Amen.

October 12

Saint Seraphin of Montegranaro

(1540–October 12, 1604)

Feast Day: October 12

Felix was born to poor parents in central Italy. His father did stonework as a mason. Felix became a shepherd, which he enjoyed because it gave him time to pray. He was not educated and could not read or write. When his parents died, his older brother, who was also a stonemason, tried to teach Felix the trade. But he had a hard time learning it. His brother would get angry and shout at him and mistreat him. Felix suffered a lot from this. When he was sixteen, he tried to enter the Capuchin Order, but they asked him to wait. Two years later they accepted him. Felix told them that he had nothing but a crucifix and a rosary. But with those, he wanted to contribute to the Order and become a saint. He was then given the name Seraphin.

Seraphin was known for his simplicity. He wore old, patched clothes and lived a life of great poverty. He was also very obedient and showed charity to all. He once said that if anyone gave him trouble, he would pray a Rosary for that person. He was convinced that Jesus gave him many graces because of that. He was assigned to be the porter for many years. As porter, he took care of people who came to the door of the monastery. Sometimes they would come at all hours of the night. But Seraphin always greeted them with great kindness and gave them food and shelter. He also would spend long hours praying during the night.

Even though Seraphin was uneducated, he had a great deal of wisdom that came from the Holy Spirit. People would come to him for advice. Even the bishop visited him once.

God gave Seraphin the gift of healing, and many sick people regained their health through his prayers. Seraphin spent his whole life doing these simple tasks. When he died, all the people in his town said he was a saint.

Saint Seraphin, your life was filled with tasks that might have seemed unimportant. But you did them with great love and that is how you became a saint. Pray for us that we might offer everything in our lives to Jesus, no matter how small it might seem. Amen.

October 13
Saint Edward the Confessor
(c. 1003–January 5, 1066)

Feast Day: October 13

Patron of England

Edward was the son of the English King Ethelred II. Because of enemies in his own country, he had to live in Normandy, France, from the time he was ten until he was forty years old. However, when he came back to rule, all the people welcomed him with great joy.

Edward prayed regularly and went to daily Mass. His trust in God helped make him a better king. He always tried to rule through diplomacy instead of war. If an argument could be settled without fighting, Edward did his best to make peace with those who opposed him. He was a gentle, kind man who showed special charity to the poor and to foreigners. He made sure that the people did not have to pay harsh taxes. He also helped monks in every way he could. He was just and fair toward everyone, rich and poor alike. This was what made Edward so popular with the English people.

Although he was a king with great power, Edward showed his honesty by the way he kept his word. While he was still living in Normandy, he had made a promise to God. He said that if his family would see better times, he would go on a pilgrimage to Saint Peter's tomb in Rome. After he was made king, he wanted to fulfill his promise. But the nobles knew that there would be no one to keep the peace while Edward was away. So, although they admired his devotion, they did not want him to go. The whole matter was brought to the Pope. The Pope decided that Edward should stay home and fulfill his promise another way. He asked Edward to give money to the poor and repair a monastery in honor of Saint Peter instead.

Edward obediently carried out the Pope's decision. Not long after the magnificent monastery was finished, Edward died. The people lovingly buried him in the monastery he had rebuilt. Edward became known as the "Confessor" because he was never afraid to confess his faith in Jesus and the Church.

Saint Edward, you did your best to keep your promises. Help me to be honest with others. May I take the promises I make seriously and be careful not to exaggerate stories or tell little lies. Amen.

October 14
Saint Callistus I
(c. 160–c. 223)

Feast Day: October 14

Patron of cemetery workers

This great Pope and martyr lived in the first part of the third century. He was once a young slave in Rome who got into serious trouble. His master, a Christian, had put him in charge of a bank. Somehow, Callistus lost the money other Christians had deposited with him. In fear, he ran away from Rome. He jumped into the sea to try to get away, but he was caught. His sentence was a terrible one: he was chained and put to hard labor in a mill.

After a while, Callistus was released from his punishment. But then he was arrested again, this time for getting into a fight. He was sent to the mines of Sardinia, an island off the coast of Italy. When the emperor freed all the Christians who had been condemned to those mines, Callistus was freed, too. From that time on, things began to go better for him.

Saint Zephrinus, the Pope, came to know and trust the freed slave. He placed Callistus in charge of the public Christian cemetery in Rome. This cemetery is now named after Saint Callistus himself. Many popes were buried in it. Callistus proved himself worthy of the Pope's confidence. Zephrinus decided to ordain Callistus and make him his friend and advisor.

Later on, Callistus himself became Pope. He worked hard to defend the true teachings about Jesus. Some people complained that he showed too much mercy to sinners.

However, Callistus ruled that even murderers could receive communion again if they showed they were truly sorry for their sins. He knew that God does not hold our sins against us if we confess them and are really sorry for them. He wanted the people to remember that God is loving and forgiving, and so we should be, too.

Callistus had been the Pope for about five years when he died as a martyr, giving his life up for the faith.

Saint Callistus, you knew from personal experience that God is merciful and wants to forgive our sins. When we sin or make the wrong choices, remind us to ask God for forgiveness. Help us to appreciate the sacrament of Reconciliation and confess our sins when we need to. Amen.

October 15
Saint Teresa of Ávila
(March 28, 1515–October 4, 1582)

Feast Day: October 15

Patron of Spain, chess players, and those who struggle with prayer

Teresa was born in Ávila, Spain. When she was a little girl in her parents' rich home, she and her brother Rodrigo loved to read the lives of the saints. It seemed to them that the martyrs got to heaven an easy way. The two children set out secretly to go to a dangerous land and die for Jesus. But they had not gotten far when they met an uncle. He returned them to their worried mother at once.

As a teenager, however, Teresa's attitude changed. She started to care only about dressing up and reading romance novels. She lost much of her love for prayer. Her father decided that she should go spend some time at a Carmelite convent. At first, Teresa was angry about this. But she eventually grew to like the nuns. At age twenty, she decided that she would become a Carmelite nun, too.

For a long time, Teresa was not a very good nun. She lived an easy life and wasted time every day in long, foolish conversations. Prayer was very difficult for her, and her health was not good. But one day, in front of a picture of Jesus, Teresa felt great sorrow that she did not love God more. She started to live for Jesus alone, no matter what sacrifice had to be made. And an amazing thing happened when Teresa turned her life over to God. Her prayer life was no longer dry or difficult. Jesus gave Teresa the privilege of hearing him talk to her. She also received many other special graces in prayer.

After this, Teresa traveled around Spain to open many new Carmelite convents. These convents were filled with sisters who wanted to live holy lives. They made many sacrifices for Jesus. Teresa herself gave them the example. She prayed with great love and worked hard at the convent tasks.

Teresa was a great leader and true lover of Jesus and his Church. She died when she was sixty-seven. Later, she was declared a doctor of the Church because of her important writings on God and prayer.

Saint Teresa of Ávila, for a long time, it was hard for you to pray. When I find prayer boring or difficult, help me persevere like you did. May I always trust that God hears me and loves me, even when I cannot hear him. Amen.

October 16

Saint Margaret Mary Alacoque

(July 22, 1647–October 17, 1690)

Feast Day: October 16

Patron of devotion to the Sacred Heart of Jesus and of those suffering from polio

Margaret Mary was born in France. As a child, she was a happy girl who loved the nuns at school. But when she was eleven, she became very sick. It took her four years to get better. By then, her father had died and her family was very poor. This was a difficult time for her, but she turned to God for comfort. Then, when she was seventeen years old, things started to go better for her family.

Around that time, Margaret Mary's mother started encouraging her to get married. Margaret Mary had wanted to be a nun, but she let go of this dream for a little while to please her family. She attended fancy parties in fine dresses and met lots of people. But Margaret Mary could not forget about Jesus. She still wanted to give her life to him as a religious sister.

After hesitating for a while, Margaret Mary finally decided to enter a convent. She joined the Visitation Sisters and was a kind, humble sister. She was not perfect, though. At times, she was slow and clumsy, which made the other sisters impatient. But Jesus loved Margaret Mary very much. He began to appear to her in visions. Jesus showed Margaret Mary how much he loves all of us. He asked her to spread devotion to his Sacred Heart so that everyone would come to know his love.

Margaret Mary wanted to do what Jesus said, but it was very difficult. Many people thought she had not really seen him at all. Some were angry with her for trying to spread the new devotion. This brought Margaret Mary great suffering. Yet she still did her best to carry out Jesus' wish and God blessed her hard work. Today, this wonderful devotion to the Sacred Heart is practiced all over the world.

Margaret Mary never had good health, but she was not afraid of death. She knew that God was all she needed to be happy, whether she was on Earth or in heaven. She was forty-three when she died of an illness.

Saint Margaret Mary, you knew that nothing was more important than Jesus' love for us. Teach us to appreciate his Sacred Heart that loves the world so much. May Jesus help us to be loving like he is. Amen.

October 17
Saint Ignatius of Antioch
(c. 35–c. 108)

Feast Day: October 17

Patron against sore throats and throat diseases

Ignatius was the third bishop of Antioch, which is in modern-day Turkey. Antioch was an important city in the Roman Empire. It was where Saint Peter spent time before moving to Rome. It was also the place where followers of Jesus were first called Christians. Ignatius worked hard to be a good bishop. He loved his people and made sure that they were not confused by false teachings about Christianity. He taught them how to love God and be united with Jesus.

At that time, it was very dangerous to be a Christian. Emperor Trajan was persecuting the Church and having Christians arrested and killed. Soon, Ignatius was captured and sentenced to die in Rome. He made the long journey with a military guard. But even though he was marching to his death, Ignatius still wanted to share God's love with as many people as possible. He stopped in cities like Smyrna and Troas and was able to visit the Christian communities there. The Christians loved and respected Ignatius so much that they took turns traveling with him.

During his trip to Rome, Ignatius wrote seven letters to different Christian communities. In them, he encouraged the Christians and asked them to stay true to the teachings of the Church. These communities treasured these letters so much that we still have them today!

Ignatius would have written many more letters, but he did not have enough time. He asked his friend, Saint Polycarp, the bishop of Smyrna, to finish writing the other letters for him. Then, when he arrived in Rome, Ignatius joined the brave Christians who waited in prison. He was killed by lions in the Roman amphitheater, joyfully becoming a martyr for Jesus.

Saint Ignatius of Antioch, you made the most of the time you were given and touched many people's hearts in your final days. When I am tempted to waste time, help me to stay focused. May I use my time wisely and creatively to share God's love with others. Amen.

October 18

Saint Luke

(Unknown–c. 80)

Feast Day: October 18

Patron of artists, physicians, and surgeons

It is generally believed that Luke was a Greek doctor. He was a good, kind man who lived around the time of Jesus. Luke never met Jesus personally, but he learned about Jesus from the great apostle Saint Paul. Luke decided to become a Christian and travel with Paul on his missionary journeys. He was a great help to Paul in spreading the faith. The Bible calls Luke "the beloved physician" (Col 4:14).

Luke learned as much as he could from Paul. He wrote down their adventures and the things that were going on in the early Church. His writings later became known as the

Acts of the Apostles. This is the book of the Bible that tells us about how the Church grew and spread.

Even when Paul was in prison, Luke faithfully stayed with him. After Paul was martyred, it is believed that Luke went back to the place where Jesus had lived. There, he talked to those who had known Jesus. He recorded all that they had seen Jesus do and heard him say. According to tradition, Luke even learned some important information from the Blessed Virgin Mary herself. She told him about the Angel Gabriel's appearance to her at the annunciation, when she found out that she was going to be Jesus' mother. She also told him about the birth of Jesus in Bethlehem and the way they had to escape into Egypt afterward. Everything that Luke wrote down became another important book in the Bible: The Gospel According to Luke. Because of his writings, many wonderful details about Jesus' life were able to be remembered and shared.

We are not sure exactly when or where Luke died. He is sometimes called Luke the Evangelist because he is one of the Gospel writers.

Saint Luke, you worked hard to record the details of Jesus' life so that people could get to know him better. Inspire me to love the Bible and to learn more about Jesus' life. That way, I can love Jesus more and more every day. Amen.

October 19
Blessed Timothy Giaccardo
(June 13, 1896–January 24, 1948)

Feast Day: October 19

Joseph Giaccardo was born in Narzole, Italy. His parents were hardworking farm people. They loved their Catholic faith and shared it with their son. Joseph prayed to Jesus in the Eucharist and to Mary. He liked to keep a little statue of Mary on a ledge in his room. He was also an altar server at his church. That was how he met a young priest named Blessed James Alberione. James was impressed with Joseph. He guided Joseph in the spiritual life and helped him grow closer to God.

When Joseph was a teenager, he entered the seminary in Alba to study for the priesthood. But in 1917, he asked his bishop for permission to leave the seminary. He wanted to join the new religious community that James had started just three years earlier. It was called the Society of St. Paul. The bishop gave his permission and Joseph professed his vows in 1920. He chose the name Timothy after Saint Timothy, one of Saint Paul's closest disciples. Two years later, Timothy was ordained and became the first priest in the Society of St. Paul.

As a member of the Society of St. Paul, Timothy was a media apostle. He wrote, edited, printed, and distributed the word of God. He performed many difficult tasks for the community with courage and humility. Things were not easy for the new congregation. Some people did not understand their mission to work in the media. They wondered how priests and brothers could be publishers. Timothy helped them understand the ways that books, pamphlets, magazines, and newsletters could be used to communicate the Gospel. He also taught the new members of the community.

Timothy soon became James' closest associate. In fact, James called Timothy the "most faithful of the faithful." He wanted Timothy to take over a leadership role in the Society of St. Paul. But Timothy became very ill with leukemia. He died at age forty-nine. Now from heaven, Timothy intercedes for the Society of St. Paul and everyone who uses the media to share the love of God with others.

Blessed Timothy Giaccardo, whether we are watching television or a movie, reading a book, or using a phone or computer, teach us to use media wisely and with moderation. May it help us become better people, uplift others, and grow closer to God. Amen.

October 20
Saint Paul of the Cross
(January 3, 1694–October 18, 1775)

Feast Day: October 20

Paul was born into a family of merchants in Ovada, Italy. He was a good Christian and practiced his faith. As a young man, Paul decided to become a soldier. But after a year, he left the army. He felt that God was calling him to fight spiritual battles instead.

During the summer of 1720, Paul had a spiritual experience. He saw visions about starting a new religious order. Paul was not sure if he should trust these visions. He went to his bishop for guidance. The bishop investigated and believed that the visions were from God. He told Paul to go ahead with his special calling. So Paul spent forty days in prayer. He wrote a rule that he and the followers of his new congregation could base their life on. Then, he got to work.

Paul decided to call his new community the Passionists. He was joined by his brother John and a few other young men who were interested. Paul and John were ordained priests in 1727. Then, after many preparations, the first Passionist monastery was started. Besides the three vows of poverty, chastity, and obedience that all religious monks and nuns take, Paul added a fourth vow: devotion to the passion of Christ. Jesus' passion refers to the way he suffered and died on the cross to save us from our sins.

Paul and his followers lived a simple, poor lifestyle to imitate the way Jesus had lived. They spent time in prayer, but they also traveled around Italy preaching. They helped many people enter the Church and grow closer to God. Over the years, they established more Passionist monasteries throughout Italy.

A few years before his death, Paul worked to begin a congregation of Passionist nuns for women. They would be especially dedicated to prayer. The first Passionist convent opened in 1771. Four years later, Paul died at the age of eighty-one.

Saint Paul of the Cross, you had a special love for Jesus, who suffered and died for us so that we could be happy with him forever in heaven. Whenever I see a crucifix or a cross, remind me to tell Jesus thank you and that I love him. Amen.

October 21
Blessed Clelia Merloni

(March 10, 1861–November 21, 1930)

Feast Day: November 21

Clelia was born in Italy. When she was three years old, her mother died. Her father remarried and Clelia's stepmother and grandmother taught her about the Catholic faith. Her father was a good businessman, but he was not religious and left the Church. He hoped that Clelia would take over the family business after he retired. He made sure that she got a good education. But he had a difficult personality. Clelia's grandmother had to leave their home. Not long after that, Clelia's father and his wife separated.

Clelia turned to God through all this family turmoil and grew in her faith. She wanted to become a nun, so she entered the Daughters of Saint Mary of Divine Providence. She loved this vocation but felt a call to start a new congregation. In 1894 she founded the Apostles of the Sacred Heart of Jesus. These sisters cared for children, orphans, the poor, and the sick.

Before Clelia's father died in 1895, he had a conversion experience and left her his estate, which she used for her community's works. But about a year later, the person who was managing the money stole it. Now Clelia was bankrupt. The sisters had to go out begging for food. Then Clelia met Bishop Scalabrini of Piacenza. He helped her get a new start. He wanted to send sisters as missionaries to the Americas to help Italian immigrants there. Some sisters went to Brazil and began this new work. Others went to Boston in the United States. The community grew very quickly in the first few years.

But after the bishop died in 1905, more trials came into Clelia's life. Because of gossip and unfair complaints, she was removed as leader of the community. She prayed about the situation, and though it was difficult, she felt it was God's will for her to leave the congregation to stop any more problems from arising. Twelve years of painful exile followed. But in 1928, she asked to reenter and was given permission. Clelia forgave the people who had been responsible for her troubles and spent her final years in peace.

Blessed Clelia, your motto was "God alone." Even in your sufferings, you always said that Jesus never abandons those who trust in him. Pray for us so that when we are going through difficult times, we might trust in Jesus too. Amen.

October 22
Saint John Paul II
(May 18, 1920–April 2, 2005)

Feast Day: October 22

Patron of World Youth Day

Karol Wojtyła was born in Wadowice, Poland. Karol loved to read, play sports, and act in plays. But he also knew a lot of sadness growing up. Both his mother, Emilia, and his older brother, Edmund, died before he was twelve years old. Many years later, Nazi troops from Germany took over his country. They killed many people and forced thousands more to leave their homes. Then, in 1941, his father died. Karol felt very alone. His sadness made him want to help other people who were suffering. He felt in his heart that Jesus wanted this too. Karol decided to become a priest to help his people.

Karol worked very hard as a priest. At that time, the Communist government in Poland was trying to stop people from worshipping God. This made many people afraid to go to church. Karol told them not to fear, because God loved them and would never leave them. He served his people with energy, talent, and love. He was made the archbishop of Kraków in 1963. In 1978, he was chosen to lead the whole church as the Pope. He took the name John Paul II.

John Paul II guided the Church for over twenty-six years. He wrote, spoke, and traveled everywhere to share the message of God's love. He created a special event called World Youth Day, where he met and encouraged young people from around the world. He also worked for peace between people of different religions.

In everything, John Paul II looked to Mary to help him tell people about her Son, Jesus. John Paul II loved Mary very much. He even received a miracle from her. Once when he was greeting people outside St. Peter's Basilica in Rome, a man tried to kill him. John Paul II was badly hurt. But to everyone's amazement, he survived the attack. He forgave the man who shot him. John Paul II knew that Mary had saved his life.

John Paul II died after a long and painful illness when he was eighty-four. It was the night before Divine Mercy Sunday.

Saint John Paul II, you believed Jesus when he told you not to be afraid. Help me trust Jesus every day, just like you did. When I am afraid, remind me to turn to God. Amen.

October 23

Saint John of Capistrano

(June 24, 1386–October 23, 1456)

Feast Day: October 23

Patron of military chaplains and people who work with the law

John was born in Italy. He received a good education while growing up and became a lawyer. Then he was made the governor of the city of Perugia. When enemies of the city threw John into prison, he started to think about the real meaning of life. John's political enemies were not in a hurry to release him. He had plenty of time to realize that what mattered most was God and living a holy life. So, after he was set free, John entered a Franciscan monastery. He was thirty years old.

For John, life as a poor friar was a big change. He had to sacrifice his independent lifestyle for the love of Jesus. And he tried with all his heart to do this. After he became a priest, John was sent out to preach. He and his former teacher, Saint Bernardine of Siena, spread devotion to the Holy Name of Jesus everywhere. John preached throughout Europe for forty years. Those who heard him were moved to love and serve God better.

In 1456, the Turks surrounded the city of Belgrade, in modern-day Serbia. The Pope was worried that they would conquer all of Europe and try to wipe out the Church. He sent John to the Christian kings of Europe to ask them for help. But when they would not listen to John, John turned to the people. This poor, barefoot friar stirred up their love of God and their courage with his fiery words.

In the end, a big army of Christians came to fight at the Battle of Belgrade. But they were still outnumbered by the enemy. It looked like they were going to lose. Then John himself ran to the front lines, even though he was seventy years old! He encouraged the men to keep fighting and held up the crucifix for them to see. At this, the Christian soldiers felt braver and stronger. They fought until the enemy ran away in fear. Not long after, John died of an illness.

Saint John of Capistrano, whether you were preaching as a friar or leading an army, you entrusted everything to God. Give me the courage to do what is right and to trust God when problems arise in my life. Amen.

October 24
Saint Anthony Mary Claret
(December 23, 1807–October 24, 1870)

Feast Day: October 24

Patron of the Catholic press and weavers

Anthony was born in Spain to a family of weavers. He learned weaving, too, and was very good at it. However, Anthony decided to leave his family trade behind to become a priest. He was ordained in 1835 and served at his home parish. Anthony dreamed of being a missionary, so he went to Rome and tried to join the Jesuits. Sadly, his health failed and he had to return to Spain. But Anthony trusted God's will for his life. He saw the whole world as a mission field. So he lived with the enthusiasm and love of a missionary while being the pastor of a parish.

Anthony was a dedicated preacher. He gave conferences to other priests to help them with their relationships with God. He was also convinced of the power of the printed word. He wrote over a hundred books. But Anthony was not to stay in Spain. In 1848, he was sent to the Canary Islands. He spent a year there preaching the Good News about Jesus.

In 1849, Anthony started a new religious order called the Missionary Sons of the Immaculate Heart of Mary. They are known as Claretians today. He also began a group of Claretian nuns. In that same year, Anthony was asked to be the archbishop of Santiago, Cuba. There, he visited parishes and spoke out against social evils, especially slavery. He blessed marriages and baptized children. Anthony was always trying to improve people's situations and help them be better Christians. This made him many enemies, and he even received many death threats. But he did not stop his wonderful work in Cuba until he was recalled to Spain in 1857 to be the spiritual director of Queen Isabella II.

During Anthony's priesthood, he did much to take care of the poor. He also promoted education through establishing libraries, science labs, and schools for music and language. In 1869, Anthony went to Rome to help with an important meeting in the Church called the First Vatican Council. He died soon after at age sixty-two.

Saint Anthony Mary Claret, throughout your life you discovered many creative ways to share the faith and make the world a better place. Help me be creative in finding ways to help others and show them God's love. Amen.

Saint Richard Gwyn
(c. 1537–October 15, 1584)

Feast Day: October 17

Richard was a Welshman who lived in the sixteenth century. He was not a Catholic growing up. But as a young man, he went to college in England. At that time, Queen Elizabeth I ruled England and Wales. She did not want anyone in her countries to be Catholic. Because most people in Wales were still Catholic, the queen and her officials tried to crush the faith by cruel laws. Priests or people who were loyal to the pope were put in prison. They were often tortured and killed. Richard knew all this, but after he had finished his studies, he decided to convert to Catholicism anyway. He truly believed in the Catholic faith.

Richard moved back to Wales and opened a school. He married a woman named Catherine and they had six children together. But it was not long before Richard was a hunted man. He escaped from jail once but was soon arrested again for being Catholic. He was told that he would be set free if he denied his faith. Richard absolutely refused. Then his jailers brought him to a non-Catholic church by force. He upset the preacher's whole sermon by clanking his chains loudly. For this, Richard was punished and publicly humiliated.

More time in prison and torture followed. The queen's men wanted Richard to tell them the names of other Catholics, but Richard would not. They condemned him to die after an unfair trial. Then they brought his wife, Catherine, to court. They told her not to imitate her husband. But Catherine was not intimidated. She bravely scolded them for lying about Richard to condemn him. She supported Richard until the end.

While Richard was in prison, he wrote beautiful religious poems and songs. In them, he begged his countrymen of Wales to be loyal to the Catholic faith. They are still in existence today. Finally, after four long years in prison, Richard was martyred for his faith. The name of Jesus was one of the last words he spoke.

Saint Richard Gwyn, you were made fun of for your religion, but you would not let go of what you knew to be true. Never let us be ashamed of our faith! May we be bold, faithful witnesses of what it means to be Catholic. Amen.

October 26
Blessed Contardo Ferrini
(April 5, 1859–October 17, 1902)

Feast Day: October 26

Patron of universities

Contardo was born in Italy. His father was a math and physics teacher. From a very early age, he taught his son to love learning. As a young man, Contardo could speak many languages besides Italian. He did well in every school and college he went to. His great love for study and for his Catholic faith made his friends nickname him "Saint Aloysius" after Saint Aloysius Gonzaga, a young Jesuit saint known for the goodness and generosity of his life.

When he was twenty-one, Contardo was offered a chance to study at the University of Berlin in Germany. It was hard for him to leave his home in Italy, but he was happy to meet devout Catholics at the university. He wrote down in a little book what he felt the first time he received the sacrament of Reconciliation in a foreign land. It thrilled him to realize that the Catholic Church is really present all over the world.

By the next year, Contardo was trying to decide what he should do with his life. He did not know if he should get married or become a priest or a monk. In the end, he chose a third way. Contardo took a vow to give himself only to God. He lived that vow as a layperson; he never became a priest or a brother.

Contardo went on teaching and writing. He did not see his faith as opposed to science. He believed that knowing and loving God more would help him understand the natural world better. At the same time, he could learn about God by admiring and studying the things God created. While enjoying his favorite sport of mountain climbing, Contardo would think of God, the Creator of all the beauty he saw. People noticed that there was something different about Contardo. They were inspired by his holiness and love for God.

Contardo died of typhoid fever when he was forty-three years old.

Blessed Contardo Ferrini, you had a great love for science and the beauty of God's creation. Help us to take care of nature and treat it with respect. May the beautiful things in this world remind us of God's love and goodness. Amen.

October 27

Eleven Martyrs of Almeria, Spain
(died 1936)

Feast Day: October 10

A civil war raged in Spain during the 1930s. Certain groups that were hostile to the Catholic Church began to persecute it. During the war, close to seven thousand Catholics were martyred for their faith. Various groups of these martyrs have been beatified or canonized. The group of eleven martyrs of Almeria includes two bishops, a priest, seven Brothers of the Christian Schools, and a laywoman. The men's names are Bishop Diego Ventaja Milan, Bishop Manuel Medina Olmos, Father Pedro Poveda Castroverde, Brothers Aurelio Maria, Jose Cecilio, Edmigio, Amalio, Valerio Bernardo, Teodomiro Joaquin, and Evencio Ricardo. The laywoman was Victoria Diez.

They were rounded up and killed in the summer of 1936. The brothers all taught at Saint Joseph's School in Almeria. They were very dedicated to their students. Brother Aurelio Maria had once said it would be an honor to die for the faith. The two bishops were devoted to their people too. Father Pedro was very active and did pastoral work among the poor. He also started schools and worked hard for education. He began a group called the Teresian Association to give teachers spiritual formation. Victoria Diez was a teacher who belonged to the Teresian Association. She and some others were shot to death in an abandoned mine shaft. She encouraged the others to be brave. According to witnesses, her last words praised Christ as her king.

All of the martyrs showed great courage when they were imprisoned. They knew they did not have long to live. But they offered their lives in witness to Jesus Christ. They even forgave their murderers before being killed. The martyrs were beatified on October 10, 1993. Father Pedro was canonized on May 4, 2003.

Saint Pedro Poveda and the Blessed Martyrs of Almeria, you showed great courage in giving your lives for Christ. Help us not to be afraid to speak about our faith to others. May our lives, like yours, show others the love of Jesus who lives in our hearts. Amen.

October 28
Saint Simon and Saint Jude
(Unknown–First Century)

Feast Day: October 28

Simon: Patron of foresters, leatherworkers, and weavers; Jude: Patron of desperate situations and hopeless causes

Simon and Jude were two of Jesus' twelve apostles. Simon was called "the Zealot" (Lk 6:15) because he had so much zeal, or devotion, to the Jewish law. Once he had been called by Jesus to be an apostle, Simon gave his heart and his energy to preaching the Gospel. He loved Jesus with as much enthusiasm as he had loved the Jewish religion. With the other apostles, he received the Holy Spirit on the first Pentecost. Then it is believed that he went to Egypt to preach the faith. Afterward, he went to Persia with the apostle Jude.

Jude is sometimes called Thaddeus. The Bible calls him Judas, but this became confusing because Jesus had a different disciple named Judas who betrayed him. People did not want to get Saint Jude mixed up with the other Judas, so they shortened his name to Jude.

Like Simon, Jude was called by Jesus to follow him as an apostle. He traveled with Jesus and listened to his teachings. He also saw the miracles that Jesus performed. At the Last Supper, just before Jesus died, Jude had a question for Jesus. He asked how Jesus would be revealed to them. Jesus answered him, "Those who love me will keep my word, and my Father will love them, and we will come to them and make our home with them" (Jn 14:23). Jesus meant he would reveal himself to those who listen to his words and commandments. Whenever we do this, we show our love for God, and God comes to live in our hearts.

According to tradition, Simon and Jude traveled together in Persia after Jesus' resurrection and ascension into heaven. They told people about Jesus and the Good News that he had come to save us from our sins. Many people listened to them and converted. But others did not like what Simon and Jude had to say. The two apostles eventually became martyrs for the faith, dying for love of Jesus.

Saint Simon and Saint Jude, Jesus told you to love him by keeping his commandments. Help me to keep his commandments, too. May I be kind and loving to the people around me and try to love God with my whole heart. Amen.

October 29

Blessed Chiara Badano

(October 29, 1971–October 7, 1990)

Feast Day: October 29

Chiara was an ordinary girl born to a family in Italy. Her parents taught her about the Catholic faith and she learned it well. In her simple way, she knew how to live according to the Gospel. One time when her mother asked her to help clean up the dishes after a meal, Chiara said no. She started to go to her room. But then she came back and told her mother that she would help. She said she had remembered the Gospel story when a father asked his two sons to go and help in the vineyard. One said yes but did not go, and the other said no but then was sorry and went. The son who changed his mind and helped was the one who did the right thing (Mt 21:28–31). Chiara wanted to do the same.

When she was nine years old, she joined the Focolare Movement. This is a religious group with a mission to promote unity and good Christian living. Chiara learned many things in Focolare, especially how to have a close relationship to Jesus. She began to love Jesus more and to pray more.

One day when Chiara was seventeen, she felt a sharp pain in her shoulder while playing tennis. She ignored it, but it did not go away. It turned out to be a painful form of bone cancer. For the next year and a half, Chiara battled the cancer and was often in pain. But she offered everything up to Jesus. Even when she was sick, she thought of others. One day she spent time walking around the hospital with another teenage girl who was sick. Chiara had pain when she walked, but she still chose to help the other girl.

Chiara's bishop, Cardinal Saldarini, heard about her sickness and went to visit her in the hospital. He said he could see a light in her eyes and asked her where it came from. She told him simply that she tried to love Jesus as much as she could. Chiara was not afraid of death but prepared for it with happiness because she knew that she would see Jesus. She died from her illness just before her nineteenth birthday, surrounded by friends and family.

Blessed Chiara, you helped others even when you weren't feeling well. You offered all that you suffered to Jesus. When I have some little thing to suffer, help me not to complain but to offer it to Jesus with love. Amen.

October 30
Saint Angelo d'Acri
(October 19, 1669–October 30, 1739)

Feast Day: October 30

Patron of missionaries

Angelo was born as Luca Antonio Falcone to a poor family in southern Italy. He was a devout boy who learned his faith well. In 1684 he met a Capuchin friar who talked to him about becoming a Capuchin. Luca felt inspired by this and he entered the Capuchin Order. But he soon left because it was strict. Still, he felt attracted to the Order, and a few years later he tried again. The same thing happened and he left once more. After praying and seeking guidance, he entered a third time. He had a rough period of training because the friars tested him to make sure he was serious about his vocation. But this time Luca, now called Angelo, stayed.

He was ordained a priest in 1700. His first assignment was to preach a Lenten sermon. Angelo prepared for it well and wrote a sermon in the elegant style common at that time. He got up to the pulpit, all set to deliver it. But then his mind went blank. He stared out at the people and could not speak. Confused and embarrassed, he stepped down and had to leave. After this humiliation, he was praying back home at the monastery in front of a crucifix. He heard Jesus telling him not to be afraid, that Jesus would give him the gift of words.

From then on, Angelo resolved to preach in a simple style that ordinary people could understand. Like Saint Paul, Angelo would preach about the crucified Christ. He would always hold up a crucifix during his preaching. Angelo's preaching was very successful. Huge crowds would come to hear him speak about the love of Jesus. He urged the people to repent and turn away from sin. Angelo was also concerned for the poor and did what he could to help them. He used to tell the ruling class that they had to deal with people in a just and fair way.

Angelo died when he was seventy years old. During his life he had inspired thousands of people to have a deeper relationship with God.

Saint Angelo, you had a hard time at first in following your vocation. But even though it was difficult, you persevered. Help us to seek God's will about the path he wants us to follow in life. Pray for us so that we might consider if God is calling us to a religious vocation in the Church. Amen.

October 31
Saint Alphonsus Rodriguez
(July 25, 1532–October 31, 1617)

Feast Day: October 31

Alphonsus was born in Spain. He took over the family business of buying and selling wool when he was twenty-three. Three years later, he got married. God gave him and his wife three children. But difficult times were ahead. In a very short amount of time, Alphonsus' wife and two of his children died. Now this businessman began to think of what

God might have in mind for him. He had always been a devout Christian. But from then on, Alphonsus prayed, did penance, and received the sacraments more than he had ever done.

When Alphonsus was nearly forty, his remaining son died, too. Despite his great sorrow, he prayed and asked God for the gift of trust. Alphonsus soon asked to be admitted into the Society of Jesus as a Jesuit. However, he was told that he must study first. So he went back to school. This was very difficult for Alphonsus, but he did his best. At last, he was accepted as a Jesuit lay brother.

Alphonsus was assigned the humble job of being the doorkeeper at a Jesuit college. Some people might complain about being given this lowly work, but Alphonsus did not. He knew he could serve God and become close to him even as a doorkeeper. And Alphonsus did grow very holy. He spent time in personal prayer and made many sacrifices so that he could focus more on God. People began to notice the wisdom of this simple, unassuming brother. They would come to him for advice about spiritual matters. One of these people was the young Saint Peter Claver, who went on to be a great missionary. Alphonsus was happy to help anyone he could, regardless of how influential or poor they were.

Alphonsus loyally served as the doorkeeper for forty-six years. He died when he was eighty-five.

Saint Alphonsus Rodriguez, some people might think your job was boring or unrewarding. But you did it with your whole heart and touched many people's lives. When we have to do a task that we do not like, help us to do it with love and a good attitude. Amen.

November 1

Blessed Peter Paul Navarro, Blessed Peter Onizuka Sadayu, Blessed Denis Fujishima, and Blessed Clement Kuijemon

(died October 27, 1622)

Feast Day: November 1

Patrons of Japan

Peter Paul Navarro was from Italy and became a Jesuit in 1587. He strongly desired to be a missionary and was first sent to India, where he was ordained a priest. After that, he was sent to Japan. The situation in Japan was complex. There were few Christians. Peter wanted to show that the Catholic faith was not opposed to the good things in in the local culture. So he adopted Japanese customs in order to win over the Japanese people. This helped to make it easier for them to become Christians. The Jesuits even began to gain some vocations. Peter Onizuka Sadayu and Denis Fujishima were native Japanese who entered the Jesuits. They became catechists who helped teach the Catholic faith to people. Clement Kuijemon was a layman who also helped Peter Navarro as a catechist.

In 1614 the government of Japan told all the foreigners that they had to leave the country. Then the government started to persecute Christians. They saw Christianity as something foreign that would destroy Japanese society. Of course, this was not true. But Peter Navarro did not leave, even though he was a foreign priest. Instead he went into hiding. He disguised himself in order to carry out his priestly work. He had to celebrate Mass in secret.

For about seven years, Peter managed to work underground. Then the authorities caught on to what he was doing. Peter Navarro and his companions were arrested in December 1621. Although they were imprisoned, Peter Navarro was still allowed to celebrate the Mass one last time. The four men had the chance to say goodbye to their fellow Christians. Then they were executed together on October 27, 1622.

Blessed Peter Navarro and companions, you willingly gave your lives out of love for Jesus. Pray for us that we might spread the Good News about Jesus to those around us. Help us to love all people and to pray that they come to know Jesus and find eternal salvation. Amen.

November 2
Blessed Adílio Daronch
(October 25, 1908–May 21, 1924)

Feast Day: May 21

Adílio was the third of eight children. He was born in Brazil, but his parents were Italian immigrants. He grew up as an ordinary boy. He went to school and enjoyed sports. After he made his first Communion, he became an altar server. He had a fervent spirit and wanted to help spread the

Catholic faith. His parish priest was Blessed Manuel Gómez González. Sometimes Adílio would go on mission trips with Father Manuel.

In 1924, when Adílio was sixteen years old, the bishop asked Father Manuel to go on a trip to a remote area. There were some German immigrants living there who had not had a priest visit them for a long time. Adílio went along on this trip. They had to pass through a dangerous area. There were several revolutionary groups there. Adílio and Father Manuel stopped at a town called Palmeria, where Father Manuel celebrated Mass and the other sacraments. He even talked to some of the revolutionaries about converting their hearts. The men rejected this and grew angry at the priest. Father Manuel also buried some people who had been killed by the rebels, giving them Christian funerals. This made the men even more angry at him.

He and Adílio continued their journey and stopped at a town called Braga. Some soldiers were there waiting for them. Father Manuel asked them for directions and the soldiers said they would take them where they needed to go. But it was a trap. They brought Father Manuel and Adílio into the forest. Then they tied them to separate trees and shot them. Father Manuel and Adílio were martyrs because they had been killed out of hatred for the Catholic faith.

Blessed Adílio, you were an ordinary boy who loved life. Yet you also had a great love for Jesus and wanted everyone to know about him. This led you to sacrifice your life for him. Pray for us that we might have courage like you and do everything out of love for Jesus. Amen.

November 3

Saint Martin de Porres

(December 9, 1579–November 3, 1639)

Feast Day: November 3

Patron of Peru, hairdressers, and social and interracial justice

Martin was born in Lima, Peru. His father was a knight from Spain. His mother was a freed slave from Panama. His father wanted very little to do with Martin and his family. He left Martin and his mother and sister without support. They were very, very poor. But being poor did not bother Martin. He grew up good and devout. He was sent to learn the trade of a barber. In those days, barbers were similar to doctors, so he also learned about medicine and how to cure diseases.

However, Martin did not just want to be a barber. He wanted to give himself to God as a Dominican brother, so he joined the Dominican Order in Lima. Martin soon proved to be a wonderful religious. No one was kinder, holier, or more obedient. Before long, God began to work miracles through him, too. He cured so many sick people that everyone in the city of Lima would send for Martin when there was sickness. He would go to anyone who needed help, regardless of their racial or ethnic background. He loved all people as his brothers and sisters in Christ. Great sums of money were given to Martin for his charities. People recognized how well he could organize works of charity. He saw to it that poor people were helped and orphans were taken care of. He also ministered to the slaves brought from Africa.

Not even animals were forgotten by this kindhearted saint. Martin used to let mice and rats come and go in the kitchen because he worried that they did not have enough to eat. In his sister's house, he took care of stray cats and dogs.

When Martin died, he was carried to his tomb by bishops and noblemen. They wanted to honor the humble and holy brother. After his death, many miracles continued to happen through his intercession.

Saint Martin de Porres, you loved all the people God put in your path, no matter what they looked like or where they came from. Help us to love others without prejudice, too. Amen.

November 4

Saint Charles Borromeo
(October 2, 1538–November 3, 1584)

Feast Day: November 4

Patron of catechists, seminarians, and against stomach diseases

Charles was the son of a rich Italian count. When he was twelve years old, he decided he wanted to spend his life serving God and the Church. Charles seemed to be a slow student because he had a speech impediment, but he worked hard in school and did well. He eventually graduated from the University of Pavia.

When Charles was twenty-one, his uncle became the Pope. He trusted Charles and saw that he was a good man, so he gave him many important duties. Charles managed to handle these responsibilities well. He prayed a lot and tried to let the Holy Spirit guide him in his work. Charles was worried that the fame and success of his position would make him proud. So he was careful to deny himself many pleasures and made an extra effort to be humble and patient.

As a priest, and later as a cardinal and the archbishop of Milan, Charles was a model for his people. He gave away great amounts of money to the poor and did not keep rich clothes for himself. He made sure that Church ceremonies were beautiful and dignified. By wise laws, gentle kindness, and his own marvelous example, Charles made his diocese a model for the whole Church. He worked hard to reform the Church and put an end to all forms of corruption. He also founded many seminaries and schools for priests. He was never a good speaker, but people listened to him anyway. They knew he was a holy man.

When a terrible disease caused many deaths in Milan, Charles did everything he could to take care of his people. He prayed and did penance. He organized groups to tend to the sick and went into debt to feed the hungry. He even had altars set up in the streets so that the sick people could attend Mass from their windows.

Eventually, Charles became very ill, worn out by his work. He died peacefully in 1584, eager to see God in heaven.

Saint Charles Borromeo, you were given many responsibilities during your life. But you trusted God and tried your hardest and that was enough. When I have chores or schoolwork to do, help me remember to ask God for help and give it my best effort. Amen.

November 5
Blessed Mariano de la Mata Aparício
(December 31, 1905–April 5, 1983)

Feast Day: April 5

Patron of missionaries and for the healing of cancer

Mariano was born into a devout Catholic family in Spain. He was one of eight children. Three of his older brothers entered the Order of Saint Augustine. Mariano followed in their footsteps and entered that order in 1921. He made his profession of vows in 1927 and was ordained a priest three years later.

He was soon sent to Brazil as a missionary. Once there, Mariano worked as a parish priest for about two years. After that, he was assigned to teach natural sciences at Saint Augustine College. He spent most of his life teaching. He excelled at this and his students liked him. He cared about his students and even visited them if they became seriously ill. He would help them keep up with their lessons, even though they could not go to school, so that they would not fall behind.

Besides teaching, Mariano was a good spiritual director. People would come to him for advice about their relationships with God. He also worked to help the poor. He organized over two hundred Saint Rita Workshops. These were groups that employed people to make good clothing that the poor could afford. Mariano would visit the people in the groups and give them spiritual conferences and guidance. He tried to meet both their spiritual and material needs. With his big smile and friendly manner, the people felt at ease with him.

Mariano loved nature and praised God for its beauty. Like Saint Francis of Assisi, he cared about animals. He also enjoyed stamp collecting as a hobby. But most of all, he had a great devotion to Mary and to Jesus in the Holy Eucharist. Mariano dedicated much of his time to prayer.

In early 1983, he developed pancreatic cancer. Despite treatment, the disease spread quickly and he died within a few months. Mariano was beatified in 2006.

Blessed Mariano, you were a saint who did ordinary things with great love. Pray for us, that in our daily lives we may praise God for all the gifts he has bestowed on us and share them with others. Amen.

November 6
Saint Laura of Saint Catherine of Siena
(May 26, 1874–October 21, 1949)

Feast Day: October 21

Patron of Colombia and native peoples

Laura Montoya is the first canonized saint from Colombia. Her father died when she was two, and her mother was left without much money. She had to send Laura to live with her grandmother. But this was difficult for Laura. She suffered from a lack of affection and felt like an orphan. Then an aunt who was a nun enrolled her in a school where she trained to become a teacher. Even though she had never been to school before, she did very well. After graduating in 1893, she taught in rural areas where the native peoples lived. Her heart went out to them. She wanted to tell them about Jesus and the Good News of the Gospel. Most of them had never heard of Jesus.

Laura was very devoted to prayer and to the Holy Eucharist. At first, she thought about becoming a Carmelite sister. But her desire to help the native peoples gave her a new idea. She would start a religious congregation devoted to teaching and helping them. She went to the bishop and asked for his advice. He gave Laura his approval. In 1914 she founded the Congregation of the Missionary Sisters of the Immaculate Virgin Mary and Saint Catherine of Siena. She and a few other women went to live in a remote area called Dabeiba with the native peoples, teaching them about Jesus. Laura thought it was very important that they teach not only with their words, but also with the loving way that they lived.

However, not everyone understood what Laura was doing. Even in the Church, some people looked down on the native South Americans. They thought that Laura was wasting her time. But Laura ignored them and completely dedicated herself to serving the people of Dabeiba. Slowly her congregation grew and flourished.

In her last years, Laura had a painful illness. For nine years she had to be in a wheelchair. But she continued to inspire her sisters with her holiness and prayer. Laura was canonized by Pope Francis on May 12, 2013.

Saint Laura Montoya, pray for us that our hearts, like yours, may be filled with the love of Christ. Help us to turn away from sin so that we may radiate Christ to all whom we meet. Amen.

November 7
Saint Willibrord
(c. 658–November 7, 739)

Feast Day: November 7

Patron of Luxembourg, the Netherlands, and people with epilepsy

Willibrord was born in Northumbria, England. His father, Wilgils, was a convert to Christianity and eventually became a saint, too. When Willibrord was still a boy, his father brought him to the Abbey of Ripon. At that time, it was common to bring boys to a monastery for their education. It was like a boarding school. When he was a little older,

Willibrord decided to become a monk. He entered the Benedictine Order and was sent to Ireland, where he spent twelve years in study and prayer.

Saint Egbert, the abbot in charge, sent Willibrord and eleven other monks to preach the Gospel in Frisia (what is now parts of the Netherlands, Denmark, and Germany). Willibrord obeyed, but first he went to Rome to get the Pope's blessing on his missionary work. The mission to Frisia was successful. The monks converted many people and built churches. In 695 Willibrord went to Rome again and the Pope made him a bishop. Then Willibrord founded the Abbey of Echternach in Luxembourg. This became a famous monastery, known for its great learning and culture.

Things were going well. But in 716 a new king who wanted to keep the old religion took power in Frisia. He destroyed many churches. Willibrord and the monks had to flee to safety. Three years later the king died and they were able to return. They rebuilt the churches and were more successful than before. Other missionaries came to the area. Saint Boniface joined Willibrord for three years before going to Germany.

For the rest of his life, Willibrord continued to preach and spread the Gospel. He also started schools to help educate the people. He died of natural causes after a long life spent serving Jesus and the Church.

Saint Willibrord, you did not become discouraged when the king destroyed your work. Instead, you waited for the right time and began again. Pray for us that we might not get discouraged with the problems in our lives. Help us to have faith that Jesus will get us through them. Amen.

November 8
Saint Elizabeth of the Trinity
(July 18, 1880–November 9, 1906)

Feast Day: November 8

Patron of those who are ill and the loss of parents

Elizabeth Catez was born in a military camp in France. Her father was an officer in the army. He died when she was seven years old. Elizabeth's mother moved the family to Dijon, where they lived across the street from a Carmelite monastery.

As a child, Elizabeth had a quick temper. As she got older, she learned how to control her anger. She learned music and was very good at playing the piano. She enjoyed going to dances and parties. But she was also drawn to God and, even as a teenager, she was thinking about giving her whole life to Jesus.

Once when she was visiting the monastery in Dijon, one of the Carmelite sisters gave her a copy of the autobiography of Saint Thérèse of Lisieux. Elizabeth read it eagerly. It made a big impression on her. She began to think that God was calling her to be a Carmelite too. She entered the monastery on August 2, 1901. She lived there only five years before she died from Addison's disease. But in that short time, she grew greatly in holiness.

While she was in the convent, Elizabeth wrote some spiritual works. She especially liked to write about God's love and the Trinity. She had a special love for the Trinity— God the Father, God the Son, and God the Holy Spirit. This is why she is called Elizabeth of the Trinity. She said that if we remember how God loves us and is always with us, this helps us love other people more, too. Elizabeth certainly lived in this love until her death at age twenty-six. Even though her final illness had been long and painful, she was excited to go to heaven and be united with God.

Saint Elizabeth of the Trinity, you truly believed that there is one God who is three Persons: the Father, Jesus, and the Holy Spirit. Help me to believe in the Trinity, too! May I experience God's personal love for me every day. Amen.

November 9

Blessed Eurosia Fabris

(September 27, 1866–January 8, 1932)

Feast Day: January 8

Eurosia was born into a farming family near Vicenza, Italy. She only had two years of school because her family needed her to help on the farm. But she learned to read and write. She read good books like the Bible and the catechism. When she was twelve years old, she received her first Holy Communion. She developed a great love for Jesus in the Holy Eucharist. She also had a devotion to Mary and joined a group called the Daughters of Mary.

Eurosia received several marriage proposals, but she did not accept any of them. She thought that God was not calling her to marriage. But then something happened that affected her life. A young woman who lived nearby died. She had three young girls, and one of the girls died shortly after the mother. The other two were still babies. Their father was away from the family, so they had no one to take care of them. Eurosia began to go to the home and care for the girls. She wondered what God wanted of her in this situation.

After much prayer, Eurosia decided that it would be best to get married. She married a man named Carlo Barban. They adopted the two girls and went on to have nine children of their own. Three of their sons became priests. Eurosia's home was also open to other children who needed foster care. She became known as Mama Rosa. Her big heart went out to everyone, especially the children of the town. She talked to them about God and helped them learn about the love of Jesus for them.

Eurosia lived an ordinary life with great love. She became holy by living well her vocation to marriage and family life. At the end of her life when she was sick, she spent even more time in prayer. She was not afraid to die, because she wanted to see God. Eurosia was beatified on November 5, 2005, by Pope Benedict XVI.

Blessed Eurosia, you opened your home to many children because you had so much love for Jesus. Pray for us that we might welcome those in our lives who need a kind word or a helping hand. Pray that we might see Jesus in each person we meet. Amen.

Saint Leo the Great
(Unknown–November 10, 461)

Feast Day: November 10

Patron of speakers

Leo was a priest who lived in Rome during the fifth century. When Pope Sixtus III died, Leo became the new pope. This happened during hard times for the Church. The Roman Empire was falling apart and tribal armies were attacking Christians in many places. Within the Church some people were spreading errors about the faith. But Leo was one of the greatest popes there ever was. He was not afraid of anything or anyone, because he knew that God was with him. He also had great trust in the help of the first pope, Saint Peter the Apostle. He prayed to Saint Peter often for help.

Leo worked hard to establish unity in the Church. To stop the spread of false teachings, or heresies, Leo explained the true faith with his famous writings and homilies. We still have many of them written down today. He called a council so that everyone would know what the official teaching of the Church was. He encouraged everyone who had believed in heresies to give them up and believe in the truth. Many people did repent and come back to the Church.

Leo also dealt with complex political situations. He did everything he could to protect Rome and keep his people safe. When a large army of invaders called Huns came to attack Rome, the people were filled with fear. They knew that the Huns had already burned many cities. To save the city, Leo rode out to meet their fierce leader, Attila. The only weapon he had was his great trust in God. When they met, something wonderful happened. Attila, the cruel leader, showed the Pope great honor. He made a treaty of peace with him. Attila said afterward that he had seen two mighty figures standing by Leo while he spoke. It is believed that they were the great apostles, Saint Peter and Saint Paul. They had been sent by God to protect Leo and the Christians.

Leo was the Pope for twenty-one years, until his death in 461.

Saint Leo the Great, your trust in God made you brave in the face of many difficult situations. When I am facing something scary or new, help me to trust in God and ask him for help. Amen.

November 11
Saint Martin of Tours
(c. 316–November 8, 397)

Feast Day: November 11

Patron of France, police, and soldiers

Martin was born in modern-day Hungary. He joined the Roman army in Italy when he was only fifteen. Although his parents were not Christian, Martin began to study the Christian religion. But he was not baptized until a few years later, when he was eighteen.

A famous legend tells the story about why Martin finally chose to be baptized when he did. One very cold winter day, Martin and his companions came upon a beggar at the gate of the city of Amiens, France. The man was wearing nothing but rags and was shaking with cold. The other soldiers passed by him, but Martin felt that he had to help the beggar. Having nothing else to give the man, Martin drew his sword and cut his long cloak in half. Some laughed at his funny appearance as he gave one half to the beggar. Others felt ashamed of their own selfishness. But that night, Jesus appeared to Martin. He was wearing the half of the cloak that Martin had given away. Right after this wonderful event, Martin went to be baptized.

A few years later, Martin left the army. He became a disciple of Saint Hilary, the bishop of Poitiers, France. For a while, he worked as a missionary. Then he had to go into exile because he opposed false teachings about Jesus and tried to teach people the true faith. Martin did not mind living in the wilderness with other monks, though. It gave him more time to pray and become close to God.

Eventually, Martin was chosen to be the bishop of Tours, France. He did all he could to convert France to Christianity. He also founded monasteries where monks could live. He prayed, worked, and preached everywhere.

After Martin's death, his tomb became one of the most famous shrines in all of Europe. People would come there to pray and ask for miracles through Martin's intercession.

Saint Martin of Tours, by sharing what you had with the poor, you showed your love for Jesus. Teach us to be generous with what we have. May we treat the poor and homeless with kindness the way you did. Amen.

November 12
Blessed Ceferino Namuncurá
(August 26, 1886–May 11, 1905)

Feast Day: August 26

Patron of Argentina and youth

Ceferino was born in Argentina. His father was a leader among the Mapuche people of South America. Ceferino was baptized by a missionary priest when he was a baby. This priest taught Ceferino about the Catholic faith as he was growing up.

When Ceferino was eleven, his father decided to send him to a military school in Buenos Aires. But the other students mistreated him because he was a Mapuche. When his father learned about this, he took him out of that school and enrolled him in a school run by the Salesian Fathers. Ceferino was a good student. Besides his classes, he also liked to play sports and to sing and dance. He was especially good at card tricks and archery. This made him popular with the other students.

At the same time, Ceferino was also growing in his faith. He loved to pray the Rosary or gaze at Jesus in the tabernacle. He was impressed by the good example of the Salesian priests. Ceferino decided he wanted to become a priest too. His father was not happy with this idea, but he allowed Ceferino to go to Italy to study with the Salesians. On his trip there, Ceferino was accompanied by Father Giovanni Cagliero, a priest who had recently been chosen to become a bishop.

When they got to Italy, Ceferino was thrilled to be able to meet Pope Pius X. He happily began his studies for the priesthood. But Ceferino was sick with tuberculosis. Soon, his illness became so bad that he was brought to Rome to recover. Sadly, the tuberculosis only became worse. Even though he was in pain, Ceferino always had a smile for everyone. He was eighteen when he died.

Ceferino was the first native person of South America to be declared a blessed.

Blessed Ceferino, you had lots of hobbies, but you especially loved spending time with Jesus in prayer. When I feel like I would rather be doing something else, help me to stay focused on my prayers. Make me as excited as you were to spend time with Jesus. Amen.

November 13

Saint Frances Xavier Cabrini

(July 15, 1850–December 22, 1917)

Feast Day: November 13 (United States); December 22

Patron of immigrants

Frances was born in Italy. As a child, she dreamed about being a missionary to China. She wanted to give her life to

God and help people who had never heard about Jesus. But when she grew up, Frances was not accepted into the convent that she asked to join, because her health was not good. Instead, she taught at a school for a while. Then a priest asked her to help out in a home for orphans. It was difficult, but Frances stuck to the work, and some other generous women joined her. Together they vowed, or promised, to dedicate their lives to Jesus.

At last the bishop told Frances to begin her own congregation of missionary sisters. Frances started at once. This congregation was called the Missionary Sisters of the Sacred Heart. Before long, it began to grow, first in Italy and then in many other countries. Frances, whom everyone called Mother Cabrini, had always had her heart set on going to China. But it seemed that God had a different plan. The Pope asked her to work in the United States instead. So Frances sailed across the Atlantic Ocean and became an American citizen.

Frances and her sisters had a hard time in the beginning. The archbishop of New York even suggested that they go back to Italy. But Frances told him that the Pope had sent her there and she must stay. The archbishop admired her pioneer spirit, and so Frances and her sisters were permitted to begin their great work for God. Schools, hospitals, and homes for children were opened up in different states. Frances and her sisters especially helped large numbers of Italian immigrants. She was their real mother and friend.

As the years passed, Frances made many trips to spread her congregation and its works around the world. There were always difficulties, but she put her trust in the Sacred Heart of Jesus. She knew that Jesus would take care of them and see that their work went well. Frances died in Chicago, Illinois, when she was sixty-seven.

Saint Frances Xavier Cabrini, your life did not go as you originally planned. Yet you trusted in God's plan and found happiness. When our plans fall apart or things do not go our way, help us to trust God. May we follow where he leads us in life. Amen.

November 14
Saint Lawrence O'Toole
(c. 1128–November 14, 1180)

Feast Day: November 14

Lawrence was the son of a chief in Ireland. When he was only ten years old, he was taken hostage by a neighboring king. For two years, Lawrence suffered as a prisoner. Then the abbot of a nearby monastery intervened and took Lawrence under his protection. Lawrence's father gratefully came to bring him home.

Around that time, Lawrence's father said he wanted one of his sons to enter the service of the Church. While he was wondering which one it might be, Lawrence told him with a laugh that he need not wonder anymore. He was happy to volunteer. Lawrence decided to stay at the monastery with the abbot who had saved him. Soon, he became a priest.

Eventually, Lawrence became the abbot of that great monastery. He had many problems to handle as head of the monastery. Some of the monks criticized him for being too strict. But Lawrence continued guiding the community in the way of self-sacrifice. He knew this would help his monks grow closer to God and he wanted to do what was best for them. He cared about the people in the surrounding area, too. When food was scarce, Lawrence made sure that no one starved. He was not even afraid of the robbers and bandits who lived in the nearby hills. He did his best to get them to stop bothering people.

Before long, Lawrence was chosen to be the archbishop of Dublin. He liked to invite the poor to be his guests. He also worked hard to keep the peace in his country and assisted Ireland's rulers with politics and negotiations. He helped many others too. Lawrence dearly loved his people and Ireland, his country.

After years of labor for the Church, Lawrence became very ill. When people asked him who would inherit his money once he died, he smiled and said that he had none. He had long ago given away everything he had to others, just as he had given himself completely to God. Lawrence was around fifty-two when he died.

Saint Lawrence O'Toole, you gave away your money, energy, and talents to serving God and others. God has given each of us special gifts, too. Help us to be generous in sharing these gifts with the people around us. Amen.

November 15
Saint Albert the Great
(c. 1200–November 15, 1280)

Feast Day: November 15

Patron of medical technicians, scientists, and the natural sciences

Albert was born in Germany. As a young man, he went to the University of Padua in Italy. There, he decided to become a Dominican and dedicate his life to God as a priest. Stories say that his uncle tried to persuade him not to follow his religious vocation. Albert did anyway. He believed that it was what God wanted. But this made Albert's father very angry. The Dominicans worried he might try to force Albert to come home. They transferred Albert to a location farther away, just to be safe. After that, Albert was free to follow his calling as a priest.

Throughout his long life, Albert was asked to fill leadership positions in the Church and in the Dominican Order. He carried these out faithfully. But his real passion was for learning. He loved to study the natural sciences, especially physics, geography, and biology. He also loved to study his Catholic religion and the Bible. He used to observe the ways of animals and write down what he saw, just as scientists do today. Albert wrote a great number of books on the sciences. He also wrote about philosophy and was a popular teacher in different schools.

Why did Albert study all these different subjects? Because he had a special love for the truth. We know that God is always true. He created everything that exists. Jesus even said, "I am the truth" (Jn 14:6). When we learn the truth about the created world, this can help us become closer to God. Albert believed this with his whole heart. He helped his students understand this, too. One of his pupils was the great Saint Thomas Aquinas. Albert guided Thomas in beginning his great works in philosophy and theology. He also defended Thomas' teachings after Thomas died.

As Albert grew older, his holiness grew. Before, he had expressed his deep thoughts in his writings. Now he expressed them in his whole way of living for God. Albert was in his eighties when he died peacefully.

Saint Albert the Great, you loved every type of learning. Please help me when I am having trouble with my studies or struggling to understand something. Remind me that everything I learn can help me know more about God and this beautiful world he has created. Amen.

November 16
Saint Margaret of Scotland
(c. 1045–November 16, 1093)

Feast Day: November 16

Patron of Scotland

Margaret was an English princess who was born in Hungary. When she was ten, she and her family moved back to England. But soon Margaret's father died. Then, in 1066, Margaret and her mother had to sail to Scotland to escape from the new king, who had conquered their land. King

Malcolm III of Scotland welcomed them. It was not long before he fell in love with the beautiful princess. After four years, Margaret and Malcolm were married.

As queen, Margaret changed her husband and the country for the better. Malcolm was a good man, but he and his court were very rough. When he saw how wise his wife was, he willingly listened to her good advice. Margaret helped him control his temper and practice the Christian virtues. She made the court beautiful and civilized. The king and queen were wonderful examples because of the way they prayed together and treated each other and their people. They fed crowds of poor people and tried very hard to imitate Jesus in their own lives. Margaret and Malcolm had six sons and two daughters. They loved all their children very much.

Margaret was a blessing for the people of Scotland. Before she came, many people had bad habits that kept them from growing closer to God. Margaret worked hard to obtain good teachers to help them change their ways. She encouraged the people to pray and spent much of her personal time in prayer, too. She and Malcolm had new churches built. Margaret loved to make the churches beautiful to honor God. She even embroidered some of the priests' vestments herself.

But Margaret had sorrows, too. In her last illness, she learned that both her husband and her oldest son, Edward, had been killed in battle. Margaret died just four days after them, hopeful that they would all be joyfully reunited in heaven.

Saint Margaret of Scotland, you were a good influence on many people because of your loving heart and life as a faith-

ful Christian. Help us to be good examples for our friends, classmates, and siblings. May our actions and attitudes inspire others to be more kind and loving. Amen.

November 17

Saint Elizabeth of Hungary

(June 7, 1207–November 17, 1231)

Feast Day: November 17

Patron of bakers, orphans, and the sick

Elizabeth was the daughter of the king of Hungary. While she was still young, Elizabeth's family arranged a marriage for her to Louis, the ruler of Thuringia (in modern-day Germany). Even though it was an arranged marriage, Louis and Elizabeth were very happy together. Elizabeth was a beautiful bride who dearly loved her handsome husband. Louis returned her affection with all his heart. He supported her in her prayer life and her efforts to help the poor. Often, Elizabeth would take bread into the streets and give it away to those who were hungry.

For six years, the couple was happy together, and God sent them three children. But then Elizabeth's sorrows began. Louis died of the plague. Elizabeth was heartbroken. Louis' relatives had never liked Elizabeth, because she had given so much food to the poor. While Louis was alive, they had not been able to do anything. Now, however, they could. Within a short time, Elizabeth and her three children had to leave the castle. Yet Elizabeth did not complain about her terrible sufferings. She placed her trust in God and prayed with even more devotion. She accepted the sorrows in her life just as she had accepted the joys.

Elizabeth's relatives took her and her children in. Her uncle wanted her to marry again, since she was still young. But Elizabeth had determined to give herself to God. She wanted to imitate the poor lifestyle of Saint Francis of Assisi. She went to live in a simple cottage and spent the last few years of her life serving the sick and the poor.

Elizabeth was only twenty-four when she died. She had great confidence that Jesus would take her to himself. Elizabeth was declared a saint only four years after her death.

Saint Elizabeth of Hungary, even though you faced suffering and sadness in life, you never lost your faith in God's love for you. When we are feeling down, help us to remember how much God loves us. Amen.

November 18
Saint Rose Philippine Duchesne
(August 29, 1769–November 18, 1852)

Feast Day: November 18

Rose was born into a wealthy family in France. As a young person, Rose often did her best to get her own way. She ordered everyone else to do what she wanted. But God was slowly working on Rose's heart. In school, her favorite subject was history. She later became very interested in stories about Native Americans in the United States. This got her thinking about life as a missionary.

As a teenager, Rose entered the convent. It was a dangerous time in France. The French Revolution was going on. Rose was not allowed to take her vows when the time came because Catholicism was being suppressed. The revolutionaries forced the sisters of Rose's convent to leave the country. Rose had to return to her family. Still, she did not give up her desire to belong to Jesus. Several years later, she joined the newly formed Society of the Sacred Heart of Jesus.

Rose's great desire was to be a missionary. However, she was nearly fifty years old before she was finally sent to the United States. In Missouri, she and a small group of sisters started a free school for the children of poor families. The work was hard, especially because of the different languages and customs the sisters had to learn. But despite the many difficulties, Rose never lost her enthusiasm.

At that time, the Midwestern United States was still a pioneer land. Rose had to travel often through dangerous conditions. Once, she nearly died from yellow fever. She overcame all kinds of obstacles to open convents and schools in Missouri and Louisiana. Then, when Rose was seventy-one, she finally had the chance to serve the native peoples who had been close to her heart since childhood. She helped open a school for the Potawatomi tribe in Kansas.

Rose was eighty-three when she died.

Saint Rose Philippine Duchesne, you were not always able to do the work you wanted to do right away. This taught you patience and trust in God's timing. When I am becoming frustrated with a person or situation, help me to be patient too. Amen.

November 19
Blessed Alberto Marvelli
(March 21, 1918–October 5, 1946)

Feast Day: October 5

Patron of Catholic Action and youth

Alberto was born in Italy at the end of World War I. From the time he was young, he was used to helping the poor. Alberto learned to see his Catholic faith in action through his parents' devotion. His mother would always give food to people who came to their home asking for something to eat. She would tell Alberto that Jesus had come to their house and was hungry.

At the age of twelve, Alberto joined Catholic Action. This was a popular group in Italy that put the social teachings of the Church into practice. Alberto also enjoyed sports, especially bicycling. He seemed like an ordinary young man, but he had a great desire for holiness. From the age of fifteen he had drawn up his own program of life including prayer times and daily Mass and Communion. His aim was to become a saint.

Alberto went to college and studied to be an engineer. In 1941 he graduated and served for a short time in the army. Dark times had come to Europe with the outbreak of World War II. His family had to move from their home in the city of Rimini to a safer place outside the city. Despite the danger from air raids, Alberto would often go into the city to help those who needed it. On several occasions, he also bravely helped in efforts to free some people whom the Nazis were about to send to death camps. Alberto broke open the sealed train cars to free them.

After the war, Rimini had to be rebuilt. Alberto used his skills to help with this. He was still a member of Catholic Action and involved in politics. He decided to run for an office himself. One night, as he was bicycling to a political meeting, a truck ran into his bicycle. Alberto died shortly after from his wounds. In his short life, he did a great amount of good, loving God through helping others.

Blessed Alberto, you saw the face of Jesus in the faces of the poor. Pray for us that we too might see Jesus in all the people we meet. Inspire us with a great desire to be holy and to love God above all things. Amen.

November 20

Blessed Maria Fortunata Viti

(February 10, 1827–November 20, 1922)

Feast Day: November 20

Patron of the loss of parents and against temptation

Anna Viti was born into a large family in Italy. Her mother worked hard to raise her and her eight siblings. She did not get much help from Anna's father, Luigi. Luigi was addicted to alcohol and gambling. He was often away from home. It was Anna who helped her mother take care of her brothers and sisters.

When Anna was fourteen, her mother died. Now Anna had to run the household. She quit school and worked as a housekeeper to support her family. She also put off her dream of becoming a nun. Anna stayed with her siblings until they were old enough to take care of themselves. Then she entered a Benedictine monastery. She was twenty-four years old. After a time of preparation, Anna took vows and received the name Sister Maria Fortunata.

Maria wanted to belong entirely to Jesus. She spent hours with him in the Blessed Sacrament every day. She loved Jesus so much that she made the devil angry. He tried to interrupt her prayer by whispering hurtful words into her ear. This was very painful for her. Still, Maria did not stop praying. She believed in God's love for her with all her heart. Sometimes she prayed so deeply, she could feel the pain Jesus experienced during his passion, when he was suffering and dying on the cross. She received marks on her legs like the ones Jesus received from the soldiers' whips. Maria offered her pain for the conversion of sinners. She shared Jesus' desire for everyone to know, love, and follow him.

Maria was a kind and encouraging woman. She lived a simple but heroic life of prayer and work. Everything she did, she did for Jesus. Her sisters knew they could go to her when they were struggling. She reminded them that suffering is only temporary. She urged them to focus on heaven and to love God and others, no matter what.

Maria was ninety-five when she died.

Blessed Maria Fortunata, you knew Jesus is truly present in the Eucharist, and you loved him with all your heart. Increase my love for Jesus in the Holy Eucharist. Amen.

November 21
Blessed Maria Franciszka Siedliska
(November 12, 1842–November 21, 1902)

Feast Day: November 21

Maria was born into a wealthy family in Poland. Her parents were not religious, so Maria did not get a good religious education. She had private tutors for other subjects. When she was twelve years old, the time came for her to receive her first Holy Communion. She met a holy Capuchin priest, Father Lendzian, who prepared her for this sacrament. He helped her to know Jesus better. Maria felt like she wanted to give herself to God. It was not clear to her then how she would do this. But she began to think about becoming a nun. When she was eighteen, she told her parents about this, but they strongly opposed the idea. So she had to wait.

When her father died in 1870, Maria was finally free to follow her vocation. At first, she joined the Third Order of Saint Francis. After three years, with Father Lendzian's guidance, she decided to begin a new order. She believed that this was God's will for her. She went to Rome, where she had a private audience with Pope Pius IX. He gave her his blessing and told her to go ahead with her plan. Maria founded the Sisters of the Holy Family of Nazareth in 1875. The community grew quickly in Europe. In 1885 Maria went to the United States with a few sisters. They began a community near Chicago, Illinois, and later in Pittsburgh, Pennsylvania.

The mission of the community was to help families live a holy life. The model was the Holy Family of Jesus, Mary, and Joseph. Just as love reigned in the Holy Family, the sisters helped families to put love at the center of their lives. Maria told the sisters that to be successful in this, they had to live holy lives themselves, centered around a relationship with Jesus in prayer.

By the time Maria died in 1902, twenty-nine different convents had been established in Europe and the United States. The sisters helped people everywhere know of God's love for them.

Blessed Maria Franciszka Siedliska, you spent so much of your life helping families grow closer to God. Pray for me and my family, so that we can live good lives and love God more every day. Amen.

November 22

Saint Cecilia

(c. 200–c. 230)

Feast Day: November 22

Patron of musicians, poets, and singers

Cecilia was a Roman noblewoman who had given her heart to Jesus. Not many details are known about her life except through stories that have been passed down about her. Beneath the rich clothes worn by women of her class, Cecilia wore a rough, uncomfortable shirt. She offered this sacrifice to Jesus, whose bride she wanted to be. But Cecilia's father said that she had to marry a young nobleman named Valerian. Cecilia was very worried; Valerian was not even a Christian. But she placed all her trust in God.

It is said that during Cecilia's wedding celebration, the lovely bride sang to God in her heart and prayed for his help. When she and her husband were alone, Cecilia gathered up her courage. She told Valerian that she was a Christian and wanted to belong only to Jesus. Valerian was stunned at first. But Cecilia soon persuaded him to be baptized. Valerian became a very faithful Christian.

Valerian had a brother named Tiburtius. He, too, learned about the Christian faith from Cecilia. She spoke so beautifully of Jesus that before long, he also decided to be baptized. Together the two brothers performed many works of charity. But it was dangerous to be a Christian in the Roman Empire during that time. The Church was being persecuted. Valerian and Tiburtius were arrested. They went bravely to their deaths rather than give up their new faith in Jesus.

Cecilia lovingly buried their bodies. Then she was arrested as well. Legend says she converted the very officers who tried to make her renounce her faith. When she was put into a fire, it miraculously did not harm her. At last, a man was sent to behead her. He struck her neck three times.

Cecilia felt great peace in becoming a martyr for her beloved Jesus. In her dying moments, she held out three fingers of one hand, and one of the other. With this, she was showing her trust and belief in the Blessed Trinity, who is one God and three Persons: Father, Son, and Holy Spirit.

Saint Cecilia, your prayer to God was a song in your heart. Teach us how to praise God with song. Help us to find good music to listen to. Guide and inspire all singers and musicians to help people with their music and make the world a better place. Amen.

November 23
Blessed Miguel Augustín Pro
(January 13, 1891–November 23, 1927)

Feast Day: November 23

Miguel Pro was born in Guadalupe, Mexico. He was a generous, courageous, and lively young man who wanted to give his life in service to God and the Church. Miguel was twenty years old when he joined the Jesuits and started his training. But the Mexican government at that time was against the Catholic Church. By 1914, the revolution had become severe and the Church was suffering persecution. Miguel and the other Jesuit novices were sneaked out of the country for their own safety. They were sent to foreign seminaries for their training.

Miguel completed his priestly studies in Spain and Belgium and was ordained in 1926. When he returned to Mexico, he saw his people being oppressed by the government. Miguel realized that he could bring them spiritual comfort. He could forgive their sins through the sacrament of Reconciliation. He could bring them the Eucharist so that Jesus could be their strength. He could also help their material needs. And that is exactly what Miguel did.

Miguel had to be very careful. He could not carry out his priestly ministry openly, or he would be arrested. He soon became an expert at disguising himself. He would dress up as a beggar or a policeman. He slipped in and out of buildings without being seen. He risked his life to meet with Catholics in secret and give them the sacraments.

Miguel performed his ministry heroically until November 23, 1927. Then he was finally caught and condemned to be killed. But Miguel never lost his courage. When he faced the firing squad that was going to shoot him, he forgave them. Then he stretched out his arms until his whole body was like a living cross. Just before he died, Miguel boldly declared his faith in Christ the King.

A public funeral was forbidden. Yet people lined up along the streets where Miguel's body passed. They stood and prayed in their hearts, thanking God for the life and witness of Miguel Pro.

Blessed Miguel Pro, you risked your life to bring people the sacraments. You knew they were God's way of giving us grace and new life. Help me to have a deeper love for the sacraments, especially Reconciliation and the Eucharist. Amen.

November 24

Saint Andrew Dũng-Lạc and Companions
(Andrew Dũng-Lạc: 1795–December 21, 1839)

Feast Day: November 24

Patrons of Vietnam

Christian missionaries first brought the Catholic faith to Vietnam during the sixteenth century. During the seventeenth, eighteenth, and nineteenth centuries, Christians suffered for their beliefs. Many were martyred, especially during the reign of Emperor Minh Mạng between 1820 and 1841. 117 martyrs are in this group remembered with Andrew Dũng-Lạc. Ninety-six were Vietnamese, eleven Spanish, and ten French. Eight of the group were bishops, fifty were priests, and fifty-nine were lay Catholics. Some of the priests were Dominicans. Others were diocesan priests who belonged to the Paris Mission Society.

Andrew's family was not Christian. They were very poor and had to move to Hanoi to find work when Andrew was twelve. There, Andrew met a catechist who taught him about the Catholic faith. When Andrew was fifteen, he decided to be baptized. After this, he became a catechist himself and taught other people about Catholicism. Others noticed his passion for the faith and ability to teach. They thought he would make a good priest. He was given the chance to study more theology. Then, when he was about twenty-eight years old, Andrew was ordained a priest.

Andrew loved being a priest. He prayed often and took good care of his parish. He led by example and gave people the sacraments. He also continued teaching and drawing new converts to Catholicism. But soon the persecution of the Church worsened. Andrew was forced to go into hiding. He and another priest, Saint Peter Thi, were arrested. Their parishioners paid a ransom for them to be set free, but it was not long before they were captured again. This time, there was no escape. Andrew and Peter would not give up their faith. They suffered tortures, but they refused to deny Jesus. Eventually, they were beheaded. They and the 115 others who were killed for their faith became brave martyrs for Jesus.

Saint Andrew Dũng-Lạc and Companions, you gave your lives witnessing to Jesus. Today, there are many places around the world where the Church is still being persecuted. Help those Christians who are under attack for their beliefs. Make me bold in living my faith and loving God. Amen.

November 25

Blessed Luigi and
Blessed Maria Beltrame Quattrocchi
(Luigi: January 12, 1880–November 9, 1951;
Maria Beltrame Quattrocchi: June 24, 1884–August 26, 1965)

Feast Day: November 25

Patrons of families, lawyers, and married couples

Luigi and Maria were the first married couple to be beatified together. Luigi was a lawyer. Maria came from a notable Italian family, the Corsinis. She received a degree in education and became a teacher. Later she wrote several books on education. She met Luigi at her parents' house and they fell in love. The two got married in Rome on November 25, 1905.

Luigi was not very religious but Maria was. Under her influence he became a more fervent Catholic. They had four children, two girls and two boys. The boys both became priests and one of the girls became a nun. When Maria was expecting their last child, she had a difficult pregnancy. Everyone was worried she and the baby would die. The doctors told her to have an abortion. But Luigi and Maria knew that was wrong and they chose life. They prayed and put all their trust in God, and a healthy baby girl was born.

The Quattrocchi home was a happy place. The family enjoyed vacations and outings and doing fun things together. It was also a holy place. Luigi and Maria went to daily Mass and prayed the Rosary with their family. They raised their children to love God. They also opened their home to others. During World War II, they took in Jews and other refugees even though it was dangerous to do so. They were active in groups such as Catholic Action and the Italian Catholic Scouting Association. They were also both members of the Third Order Regular of Saint Francis of Penance. This group was for laypeople who wanted to live the Franciscan spirit.

Luigi and Maria gave a wonderful example of how people can become holy through the sacrament of marriage. The way they encouraged their children also shows that vocations to the priesthood and religious life often come from holy marriages and families.

Blesseds Luigi and Maria, your holy family life brought joy to everyone you met. Pray for families, that all fathers and mothers may be holy and bring joy to their children. Pray also for those families who have problems, that these might be resolved through God's love. Amen.

November 26
Blessed James Alberione
(April 4, 1884–November 26, 1971)

Feast Day: November 26

Patron of those who use the media to evangelize

James was born into a poor farming family in northern Italy. His devout parents formed him well in the Catholic faith. His mother would often bring him to a nearby shrine where he first learned devotion to Mary. As a teenager, he decided to become a priest and went to seminary in the diocese of Alba.

On New Year's Eve of 1900, James stayed up all night praying. He asked himself what he could do for the people of the new century. Then he received an answer from Jesus in the tabernacle. He was given the mission to spread the Good News of Jesus by using all the forms of media available to him. James remembered this special calling in his heart as he finished seminary and was ordained in 1907. He was first sent to serve in a parish and later as a spiritual director at the seminary. Then, when the time was right, James asked for permission from his bishop to start a new work.

Gathering some young men to help, he began a small printing school in 1914. They printed Catholic magazines, pamphlets, and books. James called them the Society of Saint Paul. A year later he began a separate group for women, which he called the Daughters of Saint Paul. They had the same mission to use the media to spread the Gospel. Slowly, James' mission grew from its small beginning into a large work. These two religious orders were the first of ten institutes that he founded, called the Pauline Family.

James worked constantly, but he always put prayer first. In times of difficulty he was sustained by words he received from Jesus: "Do not fear. I am with you. From here [the tabernacle] I want to cast light. Be sorry for sin." These words are found in every chapel of the Pauline Family. They remind us that the things we do for God can succeed only with God's help and not because of our own efforts. Today, the Pauline Family continues James' vision by using all forms of media to help others encounter Jesus.

Blessed James, you were always thinking about how you could help others by bringing them the Good News of the Gospel. Pray for us that we might also lead others to Jesus, who is our Way, our Truth, and our Life. Amen.

November 27

Saint John Berchmans

(March 13, 1599–August 13, 1621)

Feast Day: August 13

Patron of altar servers

John was born to a Catholic family in Belgium. He was the oldest of five siblings. As a child, John stayed close to his sick mother, helping to take care of her. He liked to join with his friends in putting on plays about Bible stories too. He also loved being an altar server at his local parish.

By the time he was thirteen, John wanted to begin studying for the priesthood. However, his father, a shoemaker, needed him to help support the family. Finally, John's father allowed him to become a servant in the household of a priest. From there he could go to classes in the seminary.

Three years later, John entered the Society of Jesus to become a Jesuit. He prayed, studied hard, and enthusiastically acted out parts in religious plays. John never performed any great, heroic deeds. But he loved God with his whole heart. He showed this love by trying to do every little thing well, from helping in the kitchen to copying down notes for his studies.

After spending a few years with the Jesuits in Belgium, John was sent to study in Rome. When he became sick, no doctor could discover what illness he had. John knew he was going to die. Yet he was very cheerful as always. He even joked about how expensive his sickness was when the doctor ordered that his forehead be bathed with wine.

John once said that if he did not become a saint when he was young, he would never be able to become one. His intuition proved to be true. John was only twenty-two when he died. Very soon after, miracles started to take place through his intercession and people began to call him a saint.

Saint John Berchmans, you put great love and effort into doing little things well for God. Remind us that God is happy with even the smallest act of kindness. Help us to carry out our responsibilities, whether big or small, to the best of our abilities. Amen.

November 28
Saint Catherine Labouré
(May 2, 1806–December 31, 1876)

Feast Day: December 31

Patron of the elderly and the Miraculous Medal

Zoe Labouré was the daughter of a French farmer. Her mother died while she was still very young. Zoe had to run the house when her older sister became a nun. Zoe wanted to be a nun, too. However, because she was needed at home, she waited until she was in her twenties. Then she entered the Daughters of Charity of Saint Vincent de Paul. She took the name of Catherine.

Catherine had not been with the sisters for very long when she received a special miracle from God. She began to receive visions of Jesus' mother, Mary. In one of these visions, Catherine saw the Blessed Mother standing on a globe with streams of light coming from her hands. Underneath were words asking Mary to pray for us. Mary asked Catherine to make the image of that vision into a medal. She said that all who wore it would receive many graces from Jesus through her prayers.

Catherine told a priest whom she trusted about this vision. He later told the bishop. The bishop gave permission for the medals to be made. Small pieces of flat metal were imprinted with the image of Mary that Catherine had seen in her vision. They could be worn on a necklace or carried in a pocket. They became known as Miraculous Medals.

Soon, many people all over the world were wearing these Miraculous Medals. Yet no one in the convent knew that Catherine was the one to whom the Blessed Mother had appeared. Catherine spent the rest of her life doing ordinary convent tasks. She answered the door. She looked after the hens. She took care of elderly and sick people. Catherine was happy to live this quiet life. She did not want to be famous. She was only interested in serving God as best she could.

Catherine died at age seventy. Devotion to the Miraculous Medal continued to spread after her death. It is still popular today.

Saint Catherine Labouré, you trusted that Mary loved you and would bring all your prayers to her Son, Jesus. Help us to trust in Mary as our mother, too. May she bring us close to Jesus. Amen.

November 29
Blessed Bernardo Francisco de Hoyos
(August 21, 1711–November 29, 1735)

Feast Day: November 29

Bernardo was born in Valladolid in central Spain. He entered the Jesuit religious order when he was only fourteen years old. He had to get special permission to do this because he was so young. He took as a role model Saint John Berchmans, a young Jesuit who gave a great example of how to live a holy life.

Bernardo threw himself wholeheartedly into the Jesuit life of prayer, study, and action. Outwardly, Bernardo seemed like the rest of the novices who were in training. He was friendly and took part in the community activities. But in his prayer life he began to have mystical experiences. He sometimes had visions where he saw Jesus, Mary, or other saints. He never told anyone about this except his spiritual directors.

A turning point for Bernardo came in 1733. A priest friend asked him to translate a chapter from a book on the Sacred Heart of Jesus. In reading this book, Bernardo came to understand in a deeper way how much love Jesus has for us. Jesus also appeared to him in a vision and told him that he wanted him to spread devotion to the Sacred Heart throughout Spain. From that point on, Bernardo became an apostle of the Sacred Heart. He did all that he could to promote this devotion. He organized a team of Jesuits who helped inspire other Jesuits in Spain to preach about it. He wrote a book and published a novena so that people could pray to the Sacred Heart of Jesus more easily. Holy cards for the Sacred Heart were printed to hand out to everyone. Bernardo's own heart burned with a great desire to make the Heart of Jesus loved.

Bernardo was ordained a priest on January 2, 1735. He was only twenty-three years old. He was a priest for less than a year. He died on November 29, 1735, after coming down with a disease called typhus. Although he lived a short life, it was full of prayer and love. That is all that really matters.

Blessed Bernardo, pray for us so that we will have a deep devotion to the Sacred Heart of Jesus. Pray that we will trust in his love for us. Help us to go to Jesus in everything that happens, especially when we have problems and fears. Amen.

November 30
Saint Andrew
(Unknown–c. 60)

Feast Day: November 30

Patron of Russia, Scotland, and fishermen

Andrew, like his brother Saint Peter, was a fisherman who lived at the time of Jesus. He became a disciple of the great Saint John the Baptist. However, one day John pointed to Jesus and said, "Look, here is the Lamb of God!" (Jn 1:36) Andrew understood that Jesus was greater than John. At once he left John to follow Jesus. Jesus knew that Andrew was walking behind him. Turning back, he asked, "What are you looking for?" (Jn 1:38) Andrew answered that he wanted to know where Jesus was staying. Jesus replied, "Come and see" (Jn 1:39). Andrew had been with Jesus only a little while when he realized that this was truly the Messiah. From then on, he decided to follow Jesus. He became one of the first disciples of Christ.

Next, Andrew told his brother Simon (who was later called Peter) about Jesus. He became a disciple, too. At first, the two brothers continued to carry out their fishing trade and family affairs. Later, Jesus called them to stay with him all the time. He promised to make them fishers of men. After that, they accompanied Jesus on his travels and witnessed his many miracles. Once Jesus had ascended into heaven, Andrew and Peter were two of the disciples who received the gift of the Holy Spirit at Pentecost.

According to tradition, Andrew later traveled to Greece to preach the Gospel there. He told many people about Jesus and helped begin Christian communities. Eventually, he was arrested and became a martyr. He is said to have been put to death on a cross, to which he was tied, not nailed. Andrew lived for two days in that state of suffering. But God gave him the strength to preach to the people who gathered around him. Andrew was happy to spend his final hours sharing the Good News of God's love with everyone who would listen.

Saint Andrew, once you met Jesus, you rushed to tell your brother. Make us as excited about Jesus as you were. Whether we talk to people about Jesus or just pray for them, help us to bring others to Christ the way you did. Amen.

December 1

Blessed Charles de Foucauld

(September 15, 1858–December 1, 1916)

Feast Day: December 1

Patron of dialogue between Christians and Muslims

Charles de Foucauld was born into an aristocratic family in Strasbourg, France. His parents died when he was six, making his childhood difficult. His grandfather later enrolled him in a military college. Charles began to live a wild life, drinking heavily and going to parties. He gave up his Catholic faith and became an atheist. He had joined the army but was kicked out for bad behavior. After a while, he reenlisted in the army and was sent to Algeria in northern Africa. Around that time, he began to mature and become more serious about life.

Charles finished his army service and went back to France. He was not satisfied with atheism and began to search for God. He met a good priest, Father Henri Huvelin. This priest helped Charles on his journey back to the Lord. With his guidance, Charles made a good confession and received Holy Communion. That experience of God's tender mercy rekindled his faith. He completely turned away from his old life.

Yearning to do more for God, he became a Trappist monk. He lived first in France and then went to Syria. He left the Trappists to become a hermit, living a life of prayer in the wilderness by himself. Then he was ordained a priest in 1901. He went back to Algeria and built an "open monastery" that welcomed people of all faiths and cultures. He gave money to the poor and shared what little he had. He also tried to help runaway slaves. He spent his life as a witness to Jesus among the people.

Charles felt that his calling was to be a brother to Christians, Jews, and Muslims in the solitude of the desert. He wanted to be the presence of Christ to others. He had a dream to start a new religious order he would call the Little Brothers of the Sacred Heart of Jesus. However, he was not able to carry this out. In 1916 he was killed during a raid on his desert home. Later on, others started the Order of the Little Brothers in his name.

Blessed Charles de Foucauld, pray for us that we may witness to Jesus in the ordinary things that happen each day. May we live in a way that attracts people to the Lord. Amen.

December 2
Blessed Władysław Bukowiński
(December 22, 1904–December 3, 1974)

Feast Day: December 3
Patron of missionaries and prisoners

Władysław was born in Ukraine. After his mother died, his father remarried and had another son. The family had a happy, warm home. Władysław was a good student in high school. In 1920 the family moved to Poland to escape Communism, a form of government that denied religious freedom. There, Władysław studied at the university and earned a law degree. But he did not want to be a lawyer. Instead, he wanted to dedicate his life to God as a priest. He studied for the priesthood and was ordained in 1931.

Władysław happily carried out his ministry, helping the poor and the sick. But in 1940 the Communist secret police from the Soviet Union arrested and imprisoned him because he was a priest. World War II was going on at that time. In 1941 German troops came through the area and released him from prison. For the next four years he kept up his priestly work. But in 1945 he was arrested again and sent to a Soviet labor camp. Even there, Władysław secretly carried out his priestly work. He heard confessions and offered the Holy Mass in places where the guards would not see.

After almost ten years, Władysław was released and sent to the country of Kazakhstan. He spent the rest of his life there, serving the people as a priest. He would go to a different home each day to offer the Mass. Although he could have gone back to Poland, Władysław chose to stay and help the people of Kazakhstan. It was a difficult task, and sometimes dangerous. He was arrested again for being a priest and spent more years in prison. He also made eight mission trips to remote parts of the country. In one town there were many Polish people who had not seen a priest in twenty years. They were very happy that he came to bring them the sacraments.

Władysław died in 1974, worn out from work and suffering. But even during the hard times of his life, he never gave up hope, always trusting in God.

Blessed Władysław, you had a very difficult life. But you were still happy because you were doing God's work. Help us to be grateful that we have the freedom to go to Mass and receive Holy Communion. Pray for us that we will not take God's gifts for granted. Amen.

December 3
Saint Francis Xavier
(April 7, 1506–December 3, 1552)

Feast Day: December 3

Patron of Asia, foreign missions, and missionaries

Francis was born at Xavier Castle in Spain. He went to the University of Paris when he was eighteen. His roommate was Saint Ignatius of Loyola, who was about to start the Society of Jesus, also known as the Jesuits. At first, Francis did not like Ignatius very much. But soon he saw that Ignatius was a holy man and they became close friends. Francis became one of the first Jesuits and was ordained a priest.

When Francis was thirty-four, Ignatius sent him as a missionary to the East Indies. During the course of his amazing journeys in Goa, India, Japan, and other lands of the East, Francis made thousands of converts. In fact, he baptized so many people that he became too weak to raise his arms. He did not abandon the people after baptizing them, either. He founded schools and left other missionaries to help them with their new faith.

Wherever Francis went, he would try to learn the language and customs of the people he was preaching to. It was hard for him to learn new languages, but he did his best and trusted the Holy Spirit to take care of the rest. He would gather the little children around him and teach them the Catholic faith, often through songs. Then he invited them to spread the faith they had learned.

There was nothing Francis would not do to help people. One story says he once faced a fierce band of raiders, alone, with no weapon but his crucifix. They backed up and did not attack his Christian tribes. The saint also brought many fallen-away Christians to repentance. His only "tools" were his gentle, polite ways and his prayers. In the midst of his painful journeys and great labors, Francis was filled with a special joy that came from God.

Francis longed to get into China, where no foreigners were permitted. At last, the arrangements were made, but Francis became very ill. He died on an island off the Chinese coast when he was just forty-six years old.

Saint Francis Xavier, your dream was to preach to the people of China. It did not happen during your life, but now with your prayers from heaven you do more good than ever. Help all missionaries and those who have never heard of Jesus. May everyone know God's love! Amen.

December 4
Saint John Damascene
(c. 675–c. December 4, 749)

Feast Day: December 4

Patron of the arts, pharmacists, and those who write religious icons

John Damascene, also known as John of Damascus, lived in the eighth century. He was born to a good Christian family in Damascus, a city in modern-day Syria. When his father died, John became an important government official in Damascus. At that time, the emperor made a law. It forbade Christians from having statues or pictures of Jesus and the saints. John knew the emperor was wrong. He joined with many others to defend this practice of the Christians. The Pope himself asked John to keep telling people that it is a good thing to have statues and holy pictures because they make us think of Jesus, Mary, and the saints. John was good at explaining things in a way that made sense to ordinary people. He helped those who had no training in theology understand why it was not wrong to have images and statues of holy things. But the emperor still would not listen. He continued to forbid statues to be put in public places.

John opposed the emperor, bravely writing three letters. He told the emperor to give up his wrong ideas. The emperor became furious and wanted revenge. He came up with a scheme and accused John of betraying the city of Damascus. John told the people he was innocent, but he was fired from his government position and treated as a traitor anyway. Then God worked a miracle to show that John was innocent.

The people of Damascus were very sorry and offered to give John his job back. But John decided to live a quieter life where he could spend more time in prayer. He gave away all his money to the poor and became a monk, then a priest. He did many humble tasks around the monastery, helping his brother monks. He also kept on writing marvelous books to defend the true teaching of the Church. Because of this, he was later declared a doctor of the Church.

John died a peaceful, happy death in the year 749.

Saint John Damascene, you defended the practice of keeping holy pictures and statues because they remind us of God and the saints. Whenever we see a crucifix or piece of religious art, help us remember to say an extra prayer. Amen.

December 5
Saint María del Carmen Sallés y Barangueras
(April 9, 1848–July 25, 1911)

Feast Day: December 6

María was one of ten children born to a devout Catholic family in Spain. From a young age she wanted to dedicate her whole life to God as a religious sister. After she received her first Holy Communion, this desire grew even more. But she had a problem: her family had already arranged a marriage for her. That was the custom in those days. María did not let that stop her. She broke off the engagement because she was determined to become a sister.

María entered the Adoration Sisters when she was twenty-one years old. While she was there, she worked with the poor. She also helped poor women who needed training to find good jobs. She strongly supported these women, whose rights were not always recognized. But during her prayer, she felt God calling her to be a teacher. Because of this, she decided to transfer to another religious order. In 1871 she entered the Dominicans of the Annunciation, whose special work is teaching. María happily did this work for about twenty-one years.

Then she felt another call from God. She started a new order that would focus on helping needy women. It was called the Conceptionist Mission Sisters of Education, named in honor of the immaculate conception of the Blessed Virgin Mary. (The immaculate conception means that God saved Mary from having original sin even before she was born.) For the rest of her life, María dedicated herself to this work. She gave women training so they could find a decent place in society. She also helped the women to have devotion to Jesus and to his mother Mary. She died when she was sixty-three, but the order of sisters that she founded spread all over the world. María was canonized in 2012 by Pope Benedict XVI.

Saint María, your big heart went out to all people who needed help, especially the poor women of your day. Pray for us so that we can also reach out to those who need our help today. Help us remember that whatever we do to others, we do to Jesus. Amen.

December 6
Saint Nicholas
(Fourth Century)

Feast Day: December 6

Patron of bakers, children, and sailors

Nicholas was born in Asia Minor, which is present-day Turkey. Not much is known for certain about his life, except that he was the bishop of Myra during the fourth century. However, there are many legends and traditions that have been handed down about him. He loved justice and helped to free people who had been wrongly accused of crimes they did not do. He defended Church teaching and participated in an important Church council. And he loved the poor and took care of them.

One of the most famous stories surrounding Nicholas is about a poor man who had three daughters. The man did not have enough money to pay for his daughters to get married. Nicholas heard about his problem. He went to the man's house at night and tossed a little pouch of gold through the window. This was for the oldest daughter. He did the same thing for the second daughter. Each night, he slipped away before anyone could see him. But then the grateful father kept watch to find out who was being so good to them. When Nicholas came a third time, the man recognized him. He thanked Nicholas over and over again. But Nicholas asked him to keep it a secret. He did not do it for the fame; he just wanted to help the poor man and his family. Some people say that the tradition of giving gifts on Nicholas' feast day and at Christmas comes from this story. Santa Claus is a shortened form of Saint Nicholas.

Nicholas became one of the most popular saints during the Middle Ages. Even though people did not know much about his life, they knew he was a holy man who loved God. A huge basilica was built over his tomb. A large number of churches were also dedicated in his name. Today, many people still celebrate Nicholas' feast day with special traditions.

Saint Nicholas, you had a generous, loving heart. You went out of your way to help people. Teach me how to be kind and generous like you. When someone asks me for help, may I do it with a smile instead of complaining. Amen.

December 7
Saint Ambrose
(c. 340–April 4, 397)

Feast Day: December 7

Patron of beekeepers, beggars, and learning

Ambrose was the son of an important Roman government official. He was born in Gaul, an area of Western Europe that was part of the Roman Empire. When his father died, Ambrose's mother decided to move the family back to Rome. Ambrose was brought up well by his mother and his older sister, Saint Marcellina. He became an outstanding lawyer. Then he was made governor of Milan and the territory around it.

By a strange event, Ambrose the governor soon became Ambrose the bishop. In those days, the people used to suggest the name of the person they wanted to be bishop. To Ambrose's great surprise, the people of Milan chose him. He tried to escape, but it seemed to be God's will. So Ambrose became a priest and then bishop of Milan. He was only thirty-five years old.

It turned out the people of Milan had made a good choice. Ambrose became a great model and father to his people. He stood up for the Church's rights and helped make the Roman Empire more Christian. He tried to get political leaders to understand that they still had to listen to God and were not above the Church's laws. He made sure that justice was done and he protected the lives of innocent people, freeing prisoners and helping the poor.

Ambrose was also an excellent teacher. He wrote many homilies and books that we still have today. He used Greek philosophy to help people understand the true teachings of the Church. And he had a big influence on Saint Augustine of Hippo, who converted to Christianity partly because of the conversations he had with Ambrose. Augustine went on to become one of the greatest theologians the Church has ever seen. Besides all this, Ambrose loved to compose music. He wrote beautiful hymns that helped people worship God.

Ambrose died on Good Friday, the same day Jesus died, in the year 397.

Saint Ambrose, you did not plan to be a bishop. But once you knew that this was God's will for you, you put your whole heart into it. Help me to be patient and enthusiastic when I am asked to change my plans or do something I did not expect. Amen.

December 8

The Immaculate Conception and Blessed Pius IX

(May 13, 1792–February 7, 1878)

**Feast Day: December 8 (Immaculate Conception);
February 7 (Pius IX)**

Our Lady of the Immaculate Conception: Patron of many
countries, including the United States of America;
Pius IX: Patron of the First Vatican Council

The immaculate conception means that Mary never had
any sin, even before she was born. This was a special grace
that God granted to her because she was going to be the
mother of his Son, Jesus. This teaching has been held by the
Church for a long time and was already celebrated as a feast
day. But in 1854, the immaculate conception was declared to
be true without a doubt by Pope Pius IX.

Before he was Pope, Pius' name was Giovanni. Giovanni
was born in Italy. His father wanted him to become a guard
for the pope, but Giovanni wanted to be a priest. Luckily,
because of health problems, Giovanni was not accepted
into the pope's guard so he went to seminary instead.

As a priest, Giovanni did many jobs for the pope. Later,
he became an archbishop. He took good care of his people
and had a reputation for being friendly and kind. Giovanni
also worked for peace. He once convinced an army of revolutionaries to lay down their weapons. Then he made sure
that they could return home without getting in trouble.

In 1846, the Pope died. The cardinals met and elected
Giovanni to be the new pope. Giovanni knew he would have
to rely on God a lot to be a good pope. But he trusted that

God would help him and chose the name Pius IX. As Pope, Pius had to deal with complex political situations. Many countries were becoming hostile to the Catholic Church. On top of this, new types of false teachings were spreading. Pius did his best to make the truth known and help the Church around the world. He established many new dioceses and called an important Church council. He chose good leaders to help guide the Church through difficult times. Pius also had a special devotion to Mary. He wanted everyone to understand the Church teachings about Mary, including the immaculate conception. Pius died while saying the Rosary when he was eighty-five.

Blessed Pius IX, you had special love for Mary and saw her as your mother. May we have a good relationship with Mary and count on her as our mother, too. Amen.

December 9
Saint Juan Diego
(1474–May 30, 1548)

Feast Day: December 9

Patron of native peoples

Juan Diego was born in what is today Mexico City, just a few years before Europeans arrived in Mexico for the first time. Juan was a member of the Chichimeca people. They called him Cuauhtlatoatzin, which means "the talking eagle." His Christian name was Juan Diego. We do not know much about his early life. But when Juan was fifty years old, he met Franciscan missionaries who told him about God and Jesus. He and his wife were baptized and became Christian soon after.

A few years after his Baptism, something extraordinary happened to Juan. Mary, the Mother of God, appeared to him while he was walking to church one day! This was when Mary first introduced herself to the world as Our Lady of Guadalupe. Mary told Juan that she was his mother, just like she was Jesus' mother. She is our mother too. She asked that a church be built on the hill where she appeared to Juan. Juan never expected something so miraculous to happen to him. But he humbly did everything that Mary asked him to.

After Juan's encounter with the Blessed Mother, his whole life was changed. He spent the rest of his days in prayer and penance. A chapel was constructed on the site where Mary had appeared to him, just like she had asked. Juan lived in a little hut nearby. He took care of the church. He also welcomed the pilgrims that came to visit and pray there. He would show them the miraculous tilma (cloak) that preserves Mary's beautiful image.

When Juan died at the age of seventy-four, he was buried in the chapel that he had spent so much time caring for. Now millions of people come to visit the Basilica of Our Lady of Guadalupe every year.

Saint Juan Diego, you were a humble man who led a quiet life, but God had surprising plans for you. Pray for me so that I can know what God's plan is for me. Help me respond to God's invitations with joy and courage. Amen.

December 10
Saint John Roberts
(c. 1577–December 10, 1610)

Feast Day: December 10

John was born in Wales to a Protestant family. As a young man, he went to Oxford University in England for a while. Then he took a trip to France. It was there that John was drawn to the Catholic Church and decided to officially become Catholic. Afterward, John felt a strong call from God to enter the priesthood. He went to an English college in Spain and became a Benedictine monk. Then he was ordained a priest.

John's great dream of going back to England came true three years later. He and another monk were given permission to go. They knew the dangers they would meet. The Catholic Church in England was being persecuted and priests were not allowed to be in the country. John and his companion did not have long to wait before trouble began. They were soon arrested for being priests and were sent out of the country.

But John returned to England again. He worked day and night to keep the faith alive during the terrible persecution. Several times he was captured, put in prison, and exiled. He always came back to try again. The last time John was arrested, he was finishing Mass. He told the authorities that he was a priest and a monk and that he would never give up working for the salvation of the English people. They condemned him to death.

The night before he was to be killed, he was allowed to spend some time with eighteen other prisoners. Those prisoners were also suffering because they were Catholic. Even though John was going to die the next day, he was full of joy during their supper together. They told him that his cheerful courage was a good example. Everyone would know how happy he was to die for Christ and how beautiful it was to serve God.

The next day, John was executed. Many people came out to see him and were amazed at his peace and joy. Even in his martyrdom, John was a witness to the true happiness that can be found in Christ.

Saint John Roberts, your cheerful attitude uplifted others and helped them see how good it is to be loved by Jesus. Help me to smile at the people I see today. May my smile help others feel happy and loved by God. Amen.

December 11
Saint Damasus I
(c. 304–December 11, 384)

Feast Day: December 11
Patron of archaeologists

Damasus was born in Rome at a time when the Church was being persecuted by the Roman Empire. But when he was just a boy, the persecution stopped for good. The Roman Empire officially accepted Christianity as a legitimate religion. Finally, Damasus and the other Christians could practice their faith openly.

Damasus became a priest who was generous and self-sacrificing. When Pope Liberius died in 366, Damasus was chosen to be the new pope. Right away, he had a big problem to face. There was a false pope named Ursicinus. Ursicinus and his followers persecuted Damasus. They lied about him, especially about his personal moral life. Damasus had to stand trial before the Roman authorities. This caused him great suffering, but Damasus placed all his trust in God. Eventually, he was proved innocent.

During his time as Pope, Damasus built and rebuilt churches in Rome. He also worked hard to find the places where the martyrs had been buried. He made sure their graves were taken care of and wrote inscriptions on their tombs so that people would remember who they were. Besides all this, Damasus restored the catacombs—underground passages where many Christians were buried—and fixed up the Vatican's archives and historical records. He understood the importance of saving this knowledge for future generations.

However, Damasus was not only concerned with keeping the Church's history alive. He also cared for his people and their souls. At that time, there were many false teachings about the Catholic faith. People were confused about what to believe. Damasus explained the true faith to them. He also greatly encouraged love of the Bible. He asked his good friend, Saint Jerome, to translate the Bible into Latin. That way, more people could read it. He wanted everyone to be able to understand the Mass, too, so he changed the official language of the liturgy from Greek to Latin.

Damasus was around eighty years old when he died. He was buried with his mother and sister in a little chapel he had built.

Saint Damasus I, you carefully preserved the Church's history so that we could know about the early saints later on. Give us a deeper appreciation of history. May reading about saints from many different time periods inspire us to become saints today. Amen.

December 12

Our Lady of Guadalupe

Feast Day: December 12

Patron of Mexico, the Americas, and the Philippines

In 1531, the Blessed Virgin Mary appeared in Mexico and became known as Our Lady of Guadalupe. She came to Saint Juan Diego while he was on his way to Mass. Mary asked him to go to the bishop. She wanted a great church built on the very spot where she was standing. Juan was overwhelmed. He wanted with all his heart to do what the lady commanded. But how could he approach the bishop? How could anyone believe such an unusual request? Juan went to the bishop, but the bishop would not listen to him until he brought proof that the vision was real.

A few days later, Juan was hurrying along the same path. His uncle was dying and Juan was going to fetch the priest. Mary met Juan and told him that his uncle was better. In fact, Juan found out a little later that his uncle had been cured at that exact moment. Then the lady asked Juan to go back to the bishop. She wanted him to build a church. Juan asked Mary for a sign to show the bishop. Mary sent Juan into the rocky area nearby and told him to gather the roses that were there.

Juan was puzzled. He knew there were no roses. It was winter and the bushes were bare. But Juan followed her instructions and there really were beautiful roses. Juan picked them all and carried them carefully in his tilma (cloak). Then he showed them to the bishop. But that was not the only miracle that took place: Mary had also printed an image of herself on Juan's tilma! That was enough proof for the bishop. He built the church just as Mary had asked.

The timing could not have been better. Our Lady of Guadalupe appeared in the New World just when the Americas were first being explored by Europeans. Her presence helped many people come to believe in God and have faith in the Church. Centuries later, devotion to Our Lady of Guadalupe is still very popular, especially in the Americas.

Our Lady of Guadalupe, you are a gentle and good mother who knows how to speak to the heart of your Son, Jesus. Please help us grow a little closer to God every single day. Amen.

Saint Lucy

(c. 283–304)

Lucy was from Sicily, an island off the coast of Italy. We know that she was a martyr who lived during a time of persecution in the Church. However, most of the details about her life come from later legends that were passed down for centuries. According to these stories, Lucy's parents were rich nobility. Her father died when she was still young and her mother wanted her to get married. Lucy was a lovely girl with beautiful eyes. Many young men wanted to marry her. Lucy's mother chose one to be Lucy's future husband. But Lucy loved Jesus with all her heart. She had secretly promised Jesus that she would never get married so that she could be his alone.

Lucy needed a way to avoid the marriage her mother was planning. She knew her mother was suffering from an illness, so she convinced her to go to the shrine of Saint Agatha and pray for recovery. Lucy went, too. They prayed together, and God cured Lucy's mother. Then Lucy told her mother about her promise to be Christ's bride and never get married. Lucy's mother was so grateful for her miraculous cure that she let Lucy follow her vocation.

When the young man who was supposed to marry Lucy heard about this, he was furious. In his bitter anger, he accused Lucy of being a Christian. He turned her over to the authorities and she was condemned to die for her belief in Jesus. One famous legend says that Lucy was threatened with the frightening torture of being blinded. But she was even willing to lose both her eyes rather than belong to anyone but Jesus. That is just what happened. Lucy was blinded, but Jesus rewarded her for her heroic love. He worked a miracle and gave Lucy her eyes back, more beautiful than ever. After that, the judge tried to punish her in other ways, but God protected her. Finally, Lucy was stabbed to death and became a martyr. She went to heaven to be with Jesus, her true love, forever.

Saint Lucy, nothing could change your mind about loving Jesus. Help me to love Jesus with my whole heart, too. May I show that love in the way I live my life and treat others. Amen.

December 14
Saint John of the Cross
(June 24, 1542–December 14, 1591)

Feast Day: December 14

Patron of contemplatives and mystics

John was born in Spain. His family did not have a lot of money, so he went to a school for poor children and became a servant to the director of a hospital. For seven years, John worked as a servant while also studying at a Jesuit college. Even as a young man, he liked to do penance and make little sacrifices throughout his day. He understood the value of offering up sufferings for the love of Jesus.

When John was twenty, his love of God prompted him to enter the Carmelite Order and become a priest. With

Saint Teresa of Ávila, John was chosen by God to help reform the Carmelite Order. He encouraged his fellow priests and brothers to live a simple life of prayer devoted entirely to loving God. The original rule that the Carmelite Order had been founded to follow had been changed over the years, and he wanted to return to that rule.

Some people disagreed with what John was trying to do. Although he succeeded in opening new monasteries, he himself was criticized. He was even thrown into prison, where he suffered greatly. But God had not abandoned John. When these storms of trouble passed, God gave him deep peace and joy of heart. And he was not to remain imprisoned forever. He said that it was the Blessed Mother herself who helped him escape from his prison cell!

Eventually, the internal differences in the Carmelite Order got worked out. John was part of the new branch of Carmelites called the Discalced Carmelites. "Discalced" means barefoot. They were called this because of their simple, poor lifestyle. Besides helping the Discalced Carmelites get started, John had a great understanding of the spiritual life. He wrote down his wisdom in famous spiritual books that show us how to grow close to God. He also wrote beautiful poetry as the fruit of his prayer.

John was forty-nine when he died of an illness. He was later proclaimed a doctor of the Church because of his important writings.

Saint John of the Cross, you trusted God to take care of you when you were suffering and alone. When we feel lonely or misunderstood, help us to recognize God's closeness and love. May we also reach out to others who are alone or sad. Amen.

December 15
Saint Maria Crocifissa di Rosa
(November 6, 1813–December 15, 1855)

Feast Day: December 15

Paolina Francesca was born into a wealthy family in Brescia, Italy. Her father owned a spinning mill and a sawmill. But tragedy came into Paolina's life when she was just a child. Her mother died and Paolina missed her greatly. Paolina turned to prayer and found comfort in praying to the Blessed Mother. She received a good education from the Visitation Sisters, who also had a special devotion to Mary.

When Paolina was seventeen years old, she began to help her father in the family business. Her role was to give spiritual care to the girls and women who worked in the mills. She organized a women's guild, which provided retreats and prayer opportunities. In 1836 a cholera epidemic struck the area. Paolina began to nurse those who were sick. Her father was concerned that she might get sick too, but she did not. After this, she managed a workhouse for girls who were poor or abandoned, so that they could have jobs.

Paolina became friends with a widow named Gabriela Bornati. They came up with a new idea: to start a religious order that would help the sick and work with poor girls and women. They called their order the Handmaids of Charity. Paolina took the name Sister Maria Crocifissa after the Blessed Mother and the crucified Jesus. Little by little, the group attracted more members. They worked in hospitals and cared for the poor.

In 1848 a war broke out in Italy. Maria and the others went out to the battlefields and cared for the wounded soldiers. One day a group of rowdy soldiers pounded on the door of the hospital. Everyone inside was afraid the soldiers would hurt them. Maria took a large crucifix and opened the door. Five other sisters stood with her, two of them holding candles. Taken aback by this, the soldiers went away without hurting anyone. That was how Maria met all the challenges in her life: with prayer and faith in God. The Pope approved her new religious order in 1850, shortly before Maria's death.

Saint Maria, you were happy because you kept busy helping others. You also lived a deep life of prayer. Pray for us to grow in our own prayer life and to come to know Jesus better every day. Amen.

December 16

Martyrs of Thailand
(died 1940)

Feast Day: December 16

Catholic missionaries first went to Thailand (then called Siam) in the 1550s. The missions gradually spread and some of the native people became Catholics. The Catholics lived peacefully with their neighbors for a long time. But things changed in the late 1930s. The government of Thailand was at war with its neighbors. It began to see Christianity as a threat. The priests were expelled from the country.

A village called Songkhon had many Catholics. After the priest was gone, the police arrested and shot to death Philip Siphong Onphitak. He was a lay leader and a catechist who taught the faith to the people. He had been trying to stop the police from harassing Christians. The village also had a convent with two nuns, Sister Agnes Phila and Sister Lucia Khambang, who belonged to the Congregation of the Lovers of the Holy Cross. They led the Catholic community after Philip was killed. They taught the catechism to the children and were not frightened. The police told them to stop teaching. But they did not obey.

On Christmas Day, 1940, the police ordered all the Catholics to gather in front of the church. They were told that if they did not renounce their Catholic faith, they would be killed. But then they let the people go home without hurting them. That night Sister Agnes wrote a letter to the police. She bravely declared that she would never deny Jesus Christ. She said she was willing to die rather than turn against Jesus.

The next day, the police came to the convent and ordered the two sisters to go outside. The other people who were there were also told to go with the sisters. They were the cook, Agatha Phutta, and three teenage girls: Cecilia Butsi, Bibiana Khampai, and Maria Phon. They knew they were going to be killed, so they asked to go to the cemetery so they could die on holy ground. They sang prayers the whole way. When they arrived, they were shot.

Blessed Philip and the six women martyrs were beatified by Saint John Paul II in 1989.

Blessed Philip and companions, Jesus was more important to you than anything else in the world. You were willing to give up your lives to show that you loved him. Help me love Jesus as much as you did and make him the most important thing in my life. Amen.

December 17
Saint Olympias
(c. 368–July 25, 408)

Feast Day: December 17

Olympias belonged to a great family from Constantinople, a city in modern-day Turkey. After her parents died, she was taken care of by a wonderful Christian woman. Olympias had inherited a large fortune from her family. She was also both kind and beautiful, so her uncle found it easy to arrange a marriage for her when she got older. She married Nebridius, a man who had held an important government position in Constantinople. Olympias invited her friend, Saint Gregory Nazianzen, to the wedding, but he was not able to attend. Instead, he sent the new bride a poem full of good advice.

Sadly, the couple had not been married for long when Nebridius died unexpectedly. The emperor urged Olympias to remarry, but she refused. Now that her husband was gone, she wanted to dedicate her life to the service of God. And this is exactly what she did. With a number of other pious women, Olympias spent her life performing works of charity. She dressed plainly and prayed often. She gave her money away to everyone. Finally, Saint John Chrysostom had to tell her to be careful in giving away her goods. He warned Olympias to only share her money with those who really needed it. Otherwise, she would not be helping anyone.

John was the archbishop of Constantinople. He gave good advice to Olympias and her companions in their works. The women started a home for orphans and opened a chapel. They even began a hospital. They were able to help many people. Meanwhile, John became Olympias' dearest guide, assisting her in her spiritual life. When he was exiled, Olympias was very upset. She continued to support her friend, even from a distance. This made John's enemies angry. Olympias' community of widows and single women was forced to stop their charitable works. Besides this, Olympias was in poor health and was being criticized. Yet John wrote her letters to encourage her. He said God would reward her for the patience, wisdom, and love she had shown.

Olympias was around forty when she died from an illness.

Saint Olympias, when Saint John Chrysostom was going through a difficult time, you remained his loyal friend. Help me to be loyal to my friends, too. May I listen when they share things with me, be quick to forgive when we have disagreements, and avoid gossip. Amen.

December 18

Saint Peter Truong Van Duong, Saint Peter Vu Van Truat, and Saint Paul Nguyen Van Mi

(Peter Truong Van Duong: 1808–1838;
Peter Vu Van Truat: 1816–1838;
Paul Nguyen Van Mi: 1798–1838)

Feast Day: December 10 (Peter Truong Van Duong);
November 24 (general feast of Vietnamese martyrs)

Patrons of Vietnam

Missionaries from Europe brought the Catholic faith to Vietnam. The missions flourished but the Christians suffered from persecution. The persecutions came at various times; they did not happen all at once. It is estimated that up to three hundred thousand people in Vietnam were martyred for their faith. Among them were three young men: Peter Duong, Peter Truat, and Paul Mi.

Paul Mi was born in 1798. When he was twenty-seven years old, he began to serve in the missions. He became a catechist, teaching people about the faith, and began to study for the priesthood. Paul was a great, kind man and was much loved by the people. Peter Duong was born in 1808. When he was only nine, he started helping in the missions. He had two uncles who were priests. He also wanted to become a priest, but he was too young. One of his uncles started to guide him, and Peter became a catechist when he was only sixteen years old. He was known to be a very serious young man who never lost his temper. Peter Truat, born in 1816, also helped in the missionaries from the time he was fifteen years old. He was known to be very honest and kind.

A persecution broke out in the area of Tonkin where their mission was. Soldiers surrounded the village and arrested the three young men as well as the priest they were working with. They were held in a prison for a year and a half. They were mistreated and suffered a lot. But they were all very brave in declaring their faith.

Peter Truat was given the title of catechist while he was in prison even though he was still very young to have this important job. This was because he set such a good example. Other Christians were encouraged by how he, Paul, and Peter Duong trusted in God despite their sufferings. Even their prison guards were impressed by the way they stayed calm in the face of death. Finally, they were martyred for their faith, giving the ultimate witness to Jesus Christ.

Saints Peter Duong, Peter Truat, and Paul Mi, you showed great courage in giving witness to Jesus and your Catholic faith. Pray for us that we might put our faith first in our lives. Help us to also give witness to Jesus in our own way by living good lives. Amen.

December 19
Blessed Urban V
(c. 1310–December 19, 1370)

Feast Day: December 19

Patron of education

William de Grimoard was born into a noble family in France. As a young man, he decided to dedicate his life to God as a Benedictine monk and priest. At first, he was a teacher. Then he was asked to serve in leadership positions for the Benedictine Order and the Church. He was a good diplomat who helped keep the peace in Europe, especially in Italy. In 1362, William was chosen to be the new pope. He took the name Urban.

At that time, the popes had been living in a city called Avignon, in France. But the pope is the bishop of Rome, and Urban knew that his place was in Rome. He made up his mind to move the papacy back to Rome and live there. There were many difficulties. The French objected to his going, but Urban did what he knew was right.

The people of Rome were overjoyed to have the pope back. They were especially joyful to have such a holy man as Urban. He set out at once to repair the great churches of Rome. He helped the poor and started universities. He also worked hard to establish unity in the Church. Besides all this, Urban encouraged everyone to pray and live holy lives. He himself was a good example of this. Even as the Pope, Urban continued to live with the simplicity and devotion of a Benedictine monk.

Not long before his death, Urban returned to Avignon. He was sad to leave Rome, but his health was declining and he wanted to be near his family. The political situation in France also influenced Urban's decision, as did the cardinals who had been pressuring him to return to Avignon. But the people of Rome would not be without their bishop for long. The next pope, Gregory XI, was able to return the papacy to Rome for good.

Urban was around sixty years old when he died.

Blessed Urban V, you knew that being the Pope was not always easy. Remind us to pray for our current Pope often. May God protect him and guide him. May Jesus strengthen and comfort him. May he be a good shepherd of Christ's Church. Amen.

December 20
Saint Dominic of Silos
(c. 1000–December 20, 1073)

Feast Day: December 20

Patron of pregnant women, shepherds, and against insects

Dominic was born to a poor family in Spain. While he was growing up, it was his job to be a shepherd. He spent many hours alone with his sheep at the bottom of the Pyrenees mountains. It was there that Dominic learned to love praying. Soon he became a monk. He was a very good monk and was also ordained a priest.

Eventually, Dominic was appointed to be the abbot in charge of his monastery. He brought about many changes for the better. One day, however, King Garcia III of Navarre, Spain, claimed that some of the monastery's possessions were his. Dominic refused to give them to the king. He did not think it was right to give the king what belonged to the Church. This decision greatly angered Garcia. He ordered Dominic to leave his kingdom.

Dominic and his monks were given a friendly welcome by another Spanish king, Ferdinand I of Castile and León. Ferdinand told them they could have an old monastery called St. Sebastian at Silos. This monastery was located in a lonely spot and was very run-down. But with Dominic as the abbot, it soon began to take on a new look. In fact, it became one of the best-known monasteries in all of Spain. It was later renamed St. Dominic's.

Dominic loved to spend time in prayer. He grew very close to God. Because of this, God was able to work many miracles through Dominic. During his lifetime, Dominic was known to miraculously cure all sorts of diseases. But the miracles did not stop when he died. Many years later, a woman named Blessed Joan of Aza came to pray at Saint Dominic's shrine. She was having trouble having children. But after Joan prayed through Dominic's intercession, she was able to give birth to a son. When that son was born, Joan gratefully named him Dominic. He grew up to become the founder of the Dominican Order and also became a great saint.

Saint Dominic of Silos, you worked hard and persevered in doing what was right. In time, God rewarded your patient efforts by accomplishing much good through you. Help me to persevere in doing the right thing, even when I cannot see the results of my work right away. Amen.

December 21

Saint Peter Canisius

(May 8, 1521–December 21, 1597)

Feast Day: December 21

Patron of Germany and the Catholic press

Peter was born in the Netherlands. He was a very intelligent young man. His father wanted him to become a lawyer. So Peter began to study law. Soon enough, however, he realized that he would never be happy in that life. About that time, everyone was talking about the wonderful preaching of Saint Peter Faber. He was one of the first members of the Jesuit Order. When Peter Canisius listened to him, he knew that he, too, would be happy serving God as a Jesuit. So Peter joined the Order. After several years of study and prayer, he was ordained a priest.

Saint Ignatius of Loyola, the founder of the Jesuits, soon realized what a loyal and enthusiastic apostle Peter was. He sent Peter to work in many places, including Germany, Austria, and Switzerland. Peter's main task was to spread a true understanding of the Catholic faith. He also labored to bring those who had accepted false teachings back to the Catholic Church.

Peter realized how important books are and how much they can influence us. He made a campaign to stop bad books from being sold. He also did everything he could to spread good books about the faith. Peter himself wrote many works about Catholicism. These included catechisms for adults, young people, and children. His catechisms became so popular that they were reprinted dozens of times and translated into many languages.

But Peter did much more than write books. Over the years, he traveled thousands of miles on foot or on horseback. He started colleges, taught, preached, and attended important Church meetings. Some people said that Peter worked too hard. He cheerfully replied that God would help him find the time to finish everything he needed to do.

Peter was seventy-six when he died. He was later proclaimed a doctor of the Church for his important writings on the faith.

Saint Peter Canisius, you were very busy for much of your life. But instead of letting your work overwhelm you, you entrusted your time to God. When we are feeling busy or overwhelmed, help us to work hard while relying more on God to get everything done. Amen.

December 22
Blessed Jutta of Sponheim
(c. 1091–December 22, 1136)

Feast Day: December 22

Jutta was born in Germany into a family of nobility. Her father was Count Stephan of Sponheim and her mother was named Sophia. Even as a child, Jutta had a deep spirit of prayer. When she was twelve, she became very sick. She promised God that if she recovered, she would become a nun. She did get well, and a few years later, she fulfilled her promise by becoming a hermit. This meant that she lived a life of prayer and quiet, staying by herself most of the time so that she could listen to God without any distractions.

Jutta lived in a small room next to the Abbey of Disibodenberg. The room had a little window where food was passed in to her. That way she did not even have to worry about cooking or going outside to get food. Jutta gave her life completely to God in prayer and praise. This type of life was also called being an anchoress. That is because she was like an anchor holding the world close to God.

After a while, Jutta became the abbess in charge of the Benedictine abbey. At a certain point a young girl named Hildegard was brought to the abbey. Jutta became her teacher. She taught Hildegard not only how to pray, but also how to read and write and play a musical instrument. Hildegard went on to become a saint and a doctor of the Church. Since Jutta was her teacher, she deserves a lot of credit for having helped Hildegard become a saint.

It is said that about two weeks before Jutta died, God revealed the date of her death to her. She prepared for death by devoting herself even more fervently to prayer and receiving Holy Communion every day. Jutta died peacefully in the abbey and was soon honored as a very holy woman.

Blessed Jutta, your student Hildegard became better known than you. But you were not seeking earthly fame. Pray for us that we might do things not to draw attention to ourselves, but to seek the glory of God. Amen.

December 23

Saint Marguerite d'Youville

(October 15, 1701–December 23, 1771)

Feast Day: October 16

Patron of widows and difficult marriages

Marguerite was born into a large family in Quebec, Canada. Her father died when she was seven years old, and the family struggled in poverty. However, her great-grandfather sent her to school, where she was taught by the Ursuline Sisters for two years. After that, Marguerite returned home. She helped her mother keep up the household. Besides cooking and other chores, she taught her younger brothers and sisters.

At age twenty-one, she married a man named François d'Youville. It was a difficult marriage. The couple lived with François' mother, who was often unkind to Marguerite. François was involved in illegal liquor trading with some of the native people and was away from home a lot. Marguerite had six children, four of whom died in infancy. In 1730, François also became sick and died. Despite all this tragedy,

Marguerite's heart went out to those who were worse off than she was. She began to care for the poor and those who needed help.

By 1737, some other women had joined her, and they formed a new congregation called the Sisters of Charity of Montreal. They were nicknamed the Grey Nuns. Little by little, they grew in numbers as more young women joined them. Marguerite was asked to take over a run-down hospital in Montreal. She agreed, and the nuns had it repaired so that the poor could get good medical services. It was called the Hotel Dieu, or "House of God" in French.

In 1766, tragedy struck when the hospital burned down. But Marguerite was not discouraged. She knew God had a plan even if she did not know what it was. In the midst of the hospital ruins, she asked everyone to pray a hymn of praise to God. Then she raised money to rebuild the hospital and continued her work for the poor. Marguerite was able to do all this because of her great faith and love. She saw the image of God in each person, especially the poor. The Grey Nuns continued to grow after her death and spread to many countries.

Saint Marguerite, when we face difficult things in life, help us remember that God loves us and has a plan for us even when we cannot see it. Help us to be courageous and cheerful like you. Amen.

December 24
Saint Paola Elisabetta Cerioli
(January 28, 1816–December 24, 1865)

Feast Day: December 24

Costanza Cerioli was born to a large family in northern Italy. Her health was frail and she had a heart condition her whole life. When she was eleven years old, she was sent to a boarding school She stayed there for five years. It was hard because she felt lonely being away from her family. But during this time, she started to love God more and realized he would never leave her.

When Constanza was nineteen, her family arranged for her to marry a man who was forty years older than her. The marriage was difficult because her husband was hard to get along with. They had four children, three of whom died in infancy. Her last child, named Carlo, died when he was sixteen. Costanza wept greatly during his final illness. But Carlo told her not to cry because God would give her other children. That would turn out to be a true statement in the end.

Costanza's husband died later that year. Costanza was thirty-eight. Left alone with no family, she suffered from loneliness. She prayed a lot to discover what God was calling her to do with the rest of her life. As she went around the town, she noticed many orphaned children begging on the streets. Her heart went out to them and she began to help them. Soon she opened her home and took in as many orphans as she could, selling her belongings to provide for them.

Some people thought she was crazy, but slowly, the work began to grow. Other women joined her. In 1857

Costanza organized them into a new religious institute called the Sisters of the Holy Family. Like the Holy Family of Jesus, Mary, and Joseph, the sisters tried to live simply, with love, poverty, and hard work. At this point, Costanza took the name Sister Paola Elisabetta. She put the work under the special protection of Saint Joseph. She also started a congregation for men, called the Religious of the Holy Family. Her work flourished and continued to grow after she died in 1865.

Saint Paola, when you lost your family, you turned your sadness into love for others. Pray for us so that when we are sad and lonely, we can reach out to others and remember how much God loves us. Amen.

December 25
Blessed Michael Nakashima Saburoemon and the Martyrs of Japan
(c. 1583–December 25, 1628)

Feast Day: December 25
Patrons of Japan

Christianity first came to Japan in the 1540s with Saint Francis Xavier and the Jesuit missionaries. In the beginning they made many converts. About one hundred thousand people became Christians. But then the government of Japan began to see Christianity as a harmful foreign influence. Foreign missionaries were banned from coming to

Japan in 1587. Gradually the persecution grew worse. In 1620 Christianity itself was banned. A number of Christians held on to their faith and continued to practice it in secret, even though this was very dangerous. Those who were caught were often killed and became martyrs for the faith. Many of the martyrs were priests from Europe, but many others were native Japanese. The persecutions lasted up until the year 1867.

Blessed Michael Nakashima was a native Japanese who was born just a few years before the foreign missionaries and priests were forced to leave the country. He was a Catholic and he wanted to dedicate his whole life to Jesus and to serving others. He felt God calling him to become a religious brother, and he was brave enough to answer that call. Even though it was risky, Michael decided to enter the Jesuit religious order. He became known as a fervent and holy brother. He used to hide priests and missionaries to keep them safe from the persecution. This way, they could stay in the country longer and continue ministering to the Christians in Japan.

Eventually the authorities caught on to what Michael was doing. He was arrested and put in prison. They tried to persuade him to deny Jesus and stop being a Christian. But no matter what they did, Michael would not give up his faith. When they decided to kill him, Michael prayed very hard. He asked Jesus and Mary to keep him strong so that he would not change his mind about becoming a martyr. And his prayers were answered. Michael suffered greatly and willingly gave up his life to witness to Jesus. His last words were the names of Jesus and Mary. Michael had remained faithful to the end.

Blessed Michael, you did not hesitate to offer your life for the sake of Jesus Christ. Pray for us that we might realize what a great gift our Catholic faith is. Help us to live it as best we can so that we can spread it to others. Amen.

December 26

Saint Stephen
(c. 5–c. 36)

Feast Day: December 26

Patron of deacons, horses, and against headaches

Stephen's name means "crown." He was the first disciple of Jesus to receive the martyr's crown, or to die for the faith. We read about him in the book of the Bible called the Acts of the Apostles. Saint Peter and the apostles needed helpers to look after the widows and the poor. So they chose seven upright, or virtuous, men to be ordained deacons. Stephen was one of these men. He gladly accepted this ministry to be a deacon in the Church.

God worked many miracles through Stephen. Stephen spoke with such wisdom and passion that many of his hearers became followers of Jesus. The enemies of the Church of Jesus were furious to see how successful Stephen's preaching was. They came up with a plot to kill him. They could not answer his wise arguments, so they got men to lie about him. These men said that Stephen had spoken sinfully against God. But even when Stephen stood on trial in front of all these enemies, he was not afraid. God was giving him courage. In fact, the Bible says that Stephen's face looked like the face of an angel (see Acts 6:15).

After they had made their accusations against him, Stephen gave a brave speech. He spoke about Jesus, showing that he is the Savior God had promised to send. He scolded his enemies for not having believed in Jesus. This made them furious. They rose up in great anger and shouted at him. But Stephen looked up to heaven. He said that he saw the heavens opening and Jesus standing at God's right hand. But his opponents covered their ears and refused to listen to another word.

Stephen was dragged outside the city of Jerusalem and stoned to death. Before he died, he prayed, "Lord Jesus, receive my spirit" (Acts 7:59). Then he fell to his knees and begged God to forgive his enemies for killing him. After such an expression of love, Stephen went to his heavenly reward.

Saint Stephen, your ministry as a deacon was to serve others and to preach God's word. You boldly carried out this ministry with your whole heart. Help us to preach God's word by how we live. May we witness to God's love by loving others and serving them generously. Amen.

December 27
Saint John the Apostle
(c. 6–c. 100)

Feast Day: December 27

Patron of friendship, painters, and writers

John was a fisherman in Galilee. Jesus called him to be an apostle with his brother, Saint James. Jesus gave these sons of Zebedee the nickname "Sons of Thunder" (Mk 3:17). John was the youngest of the apostles. He was dearly loved by Jesus. He and Jesus were so close that at the Last Supper, John leaned his head on Jesus' chest. John was also the only apostle who stayed by Jesus at the foot of the cross when all of the other apostles ran away in fear. The dying Jesus asked John to take care of his mother, Mary. Looking at her and John, he said, "Here is your mother" (Jn 19:27). From then on, the Blessed Mother lived with John. She loved him like a son, and he loved her as his own mother.

On Easter morning, some women went to visit Jesus' tomb. They came running back to the apostles with exciting news: Jesus' body was gone. Saint Peter and John set out to investigate. John arrived first but waited for Peter to go in ahead of him. Then he entered and saw the neatly folded burial cloths. Later that same week, the disciples were fishing on the lake of Tiberias without success. A man standing on the beach suggested they let down their net on the other side of the boat. When they pulled it up again, it was full of large fish. At once, John recognized that the man was Jesus, risen from the dead!

After Jesus had ascended to heaven and sent the Holy Spirit at Pentecost, Peter and John cured a crippled man by calling on Jesus' name. According to tradition, John then preached the Gospel and eventually became the bishop of Ephesus. Inspired by the Holy Spirit, he wrote down what he remembered from his time with Jesus. This became the Gospel According to John. The three Letters of John are also attributed to him, as well as Revelation, the last book of the Bible.

John lived to reach a ripe old age. He was the only apostle who was not martyred.

Saint John, you often wrote about God's love. You said, "since God loved us so much, we also ought to love one another" (1 Jn 4:11). May I believe in God's love for me. Help me to become a more loving person by the choices I make every day. Amen.

December 28

Blessed Odoardo Focherini

(June 6, 1907–December 27, 1944)

Feast Day: June 6

Odoardo was born in Carpi, Italy. His mother died when he was just two years old. But his father remarried and Odoardo grew up in a happy home. He enjoyed life and liked to play the harmonica and go skiing. As a young man he found work as an insurance agent. He fell in love and in 1930 he got married to Maria Marchesi. They had seven children together.

To support his family, Odoardo became a journalist. He was the director of an Italian newspaper called L'Avvenire.

He also wrote for the Vatican newspaper, *L'Osservatore Romano*. For Odoardo, journalism was not just a job. It was also a way to help people understand their faith better. He was very involved in the Church, especially with a group called Catholic Action. This group organized lay Catholics to help spread the Gospel among the people and strengthen their faith.

In 1939 World War II broke out in Europe. There was terrible devastation. The Nazis were trying to kill all the Jewish people. In the fall of 1943, Odoardo began to help some of the Jews escape. A train had come to Italy carrying people from Poland who were fleeing the Nazis. Odoardo arranged to get them identification papers. He himself brought them to the border so they could cross into Switzerland. Switzerland was a neutral country where they would be safe. Odoardo did this several times and saved the lives of over a hundred Jewish people.

Unfortunately, the Nazis who were in Italy eventually found out what Odoardo was doing. They arrested him in March 1944. He was sent to various prisons in Italy, and in August he was sent to Germany. He died in a concentration camp there. Before his death, he wrote a letter to tell his family goodbye. He also said that he felt he was doing God's will. When he died, he offered his life for the Church and for world peace.

Blessed Odoardo, you lived by the teachings of Jesus who told us to love one another. You showed great love to your wife and children and had a holy family life. You also loved your neighbor by giving your own life in helping to save others. Pray for us so that we can show the love of Christ to everyone we meet. Amen.

December 29

Saint Thomas Becket

(c. December 21, 1118–December 29, 1170)

Feast Day: December 29

Patron of diocesan priests

Thomas Becket was born in London. As a young man, he worked in the household of the archbishop of Canterbury. He began studies to become a priest. Thomas was handsome, intelligent, and friendly. Before long, he became close with King Henry II. They enjoyed sports and would go hunting together.

Thomas was thirty-six when Henry made him his chancellor, which was an important role in the government. When the archbishop of Canterbury died, the king wanted Thomas to become the new archbishop. Thomas told him this was a bad idea. Being the archbishop would put Thomas in direct conflict with Henry if the king tried to do anything that caused trouble with the Church.

Sadly, Henry ignored Thomas' warning. Thomas was ordained a priest and a bishop in 1162. He gave up his rich lifestyle and started to live simply, caring for the poor and praying more. As he had feared, there was soon trouble with the king. Henry wanted to increase his power over the Catholic Church in England. He expected Thomas to side with him because they were friends and Thomas had often agreed with him in the past. But Thomas was taking his responsibility as archbishop seriously. He could not allow the king to overstep his bounds and control the Church. Instead, Thomas listened to the Pope and stood up for the Church's rights.

This made Henry furious. Thomas fled to France for his own safety. He stayed there for six years. Finally, Henry allowed Thomas to return to England. But things were still tense between the two. One day, Henry complained about Thomas to some of his knights. They took his complaints literally. Thinking to please the king, they murdered Thomas in his own cathedral. With Thomas' last breath, he said he was willing to die for Jesus and in defense of the Church.

Henry was sorry for what had happened to his former friend. He asked for forgiveness and did penance to show how sorry he was. Meanwhile, miracles began to happen at Thomas' tomb. It was not long before Thomas was declared a saint.

Saint Thomas Becket, friendship was important to you, but doing the right thing and serving God and the Church were even more important. Help us to have good priorities in our friendships. May the friends we choose help us to become better people and to love God more. Amen.

December 30
Blessed Margherita Colonna
(c. 1255–December 30, 1284)

Feast Day: December 30

The Colonnas were a notable family in Italy. Margherita could have lived a wealthy life among the rich and powerful people of her day. But she chose instead to leave all things and follow Jesus. When she was about two years old, her father died, and her mother died when Margherita was ten. From that point on her two older brothers, Giovanni and Giacomo, took care of her. When she was a little older, they thought she could find a good husband and get married. But Margherita believed that God was calling her to a different vocation. Her brothers did not object, so she was free to follow where Jesus was calling her.

Margherita went to a country house that her family owned, taking along two faithful maids. There the small group started to live a life of prayer and penance, helping the poor. They lived a lifestyle that was modeled on that of the Poor Clares, a religious order of nuns. However, they did not officially belong to the Poor Clares. Margherita wanted to enter the Poor Clares, but she got sick before she could. This prevented her from carrying out her plan. But God had something else in store for Margherita.

Margherita's brother Giacomo had become a priest and a cardinal. He was an important leader in the Church. He thought that Margherita should set up the country house as though it were a Poor Clare convent. Margherita decided to follow his advice. She and her brother went to the Pope and received permission to set up the house this way. Soon, more women came to join Margherita and her companions. They grew together in holiness, coming to love God more and more every day.

For the last seven years of her life, Margherita suffered from a painful wound in her right side that could not be cured. But she did not become bitter about this. Instead, she offered her sufferings to Jesus, in union with his sufferings. This made her closer to God than ever.

Blessed Margherita, you chose to give up the goods of this world in order to follow Jesus in his poverty. Pray for us so that we might set our hearts on heavenly things. Help us to realize that this world is passing and to think more about heaven. Amen.

December 31
Saint John Francis Regis
(January 31, 1597–December 31, 1640)

Feast Day: June 16

Patron of lace makers and social workers

John was born to a devout noble family in France. Even as a child, he loved to pray and talk about God. His classmates teased him about this at first, but eventually they came to admire him. When he was eighteen, John entered the Jesuit Order, wanting to give his life over to Jesus. After he was ordained a priest, he began his work as a missionary preacher.

John gave simple talks that came right from his heart. He especially spoke to the poor and ordinary folks. They came in great crowds to hear him. John spent his mornings praying, hearing confessions, and preaching. In the afternoon, he would visit prisons and hospitals. He also took care of orphans and women, keeping them safe and finding them good jobs. He tried to help people turn their lives around and return to God. John believed his efforts would be worthwhile if he could stop even one sin from being committed.

John journeyed up to wild mountain parishes even on the coldest days of winter to preach in the rural areas of France. He worked long hours in rain or shine. Sometimes he would start off for a faraway town at three o'clock in the morning with a few apples in his pocket for his day's food. The people who lived in those isolated areas were touched by John's great love for them and his desire to bring them the sacraments.

According to one legend, John once fell and broke his leg while traveling to a remote village. He pressed on anyway. When John reached the village, he went at once to hear confessions. He did not have time to get his leg taken care of. But at the end of the day, when the doctor looked at it, John's leg was already completely healed. God had worked a miracle for him.

Eventually, John became very ill on one of his preaching missions. Just before he died, he said that he could see Jesus and the Blessed Mother opening up heaven for him.

Saint John Francis Regis, your love for Jesus gave you great persistence in serving God's people. Help us to be as motivated and enthusiastic as you were in building up the kingdom of God. May our whole lives be centered around Jesus and the love he has for us. Amen.

Acknowledgments

Special thanks to Sister Marianne Lorraine Trouvé, Sister Amanda Marie Detry, Sister Marlyn Evangelina Monge, and Cecilia Cicone for their collaboration on this project. Without their dedication, research, and writing contributions, this book would not have been possible.

Index

A

B

C

D

E

F

G

H

I

J

K

L

M

N

O

P

W

Z

smile

God loves you